ADVA

In *Your4Truths*, Judy Kane provides examples from her own life, those of her clients, and the world of science and psychology, to perfectly illustrate each Truth and its impact on our lives. From the limiting effects of ingrained negative beliefs, to the sweet joy of releasing these beliefs, and so much more, this book is an invaluable resource and guide to living a fulfilled and joyful life. A true gem!

— NICOLETTE BLANCO, AUTHOR OF *BY A THREAD: RESILIENCE STRATEGIES FOR THE PARTIALLY UNRAVELED*

A must-read if you *think* you are doing all the right things, but you just can't seem to make progress. Through stories Judy Kane guides you to ask questions about what subconscious beliefs you may have that are holding you back or creating stress in your own life. Easy to understand discussion on topics that are sometimes difficult to work through on your own.

— CONNIE JO MILLER, OWNER ENIGMA BOOKKEEPING SOLUTIONS

After reading *Your4Truths*, I believe that anyone can attain inner peace and reclaim their lives. Understanding and choosing to clear life roadblocks can help you have an appreciation for life and to live your life to its fullest capacity. Judy, I appreciate you putting this powerful work together and sharing it with the world.

— MARLENE LUCAS

How do I even begin to capture what Judy Kane's book *Your4Truths* meant to me? Ms. Kane says, "Everyone deserves to believe these four basic truths: you are safe, you are worthy, you are lovable, and you are connected to something bigger than yourself." Can you imagine a world where everyone actually embraced these truths? It would be a kinder, more compassionate existence for sure!

While reading *Your4Truths*, so much of it resonated with me. Understanding the interplay of our ego (which is just trying to keep us safe) and the self-limiting beliefs it perpetuates to accomplish its job is critical to our ability to grow, both personally and in our business, and become self-actualized. Ms. Kane's book explains this interplay with understandable and relatable real-life experiences, both her own and those of her clients and friends. *Your4Truths* is required reading for anyone wanting to be the best possible version of themselves!

— CHERI D. ANDREWS, ESQ., AUTHOR
OF *SMOOTH SAILING: A PRACTICAL GUIDE
TO LEGALLY PROTECTING YOUR BUSINESS*

Judy does a wonderful job of explaining subconscious beliefs, where they come from, and how they impact us in our daily lives. This book is approachable, easy to read, and educational. I recommend it for anyone who is experiencing a struggle and can't seem to pin-point where it is coming from.

— SUZANNE TREGENZA MOORE, BUSINESS AND
MARKETING COACH AND AUTHOR OF *HANG ON TIGHT!
LEARN TO LOVE THE ROLLER COASTER OF ENTREPRENEURSHIP*

Judy is one of the most gracious and loving people I know. She is committed to people to succeed and pursue their dreams— right now! Through this book, she provides guidelines and exercises that are truly life changing. Judy has helped unlock my true potential through her practical tips and I highly recommend her book and consulting services to anyone with a big dream.

— JONI RAE, EXECUTIVE ADVISOR

This book is for you if you're feeling stuck and strangely resistant to the bright shiny future you can see on the horizon. It will bring clarity and help you move forward...if you're open to the message it contains and willing to do some introspection. Recognizing and overcoming limiting beliefs can change your life. I know it's changed mine!

— DEBRA CLARK, HEALTH AND WELLNESS COACH

You can change those subconscious beliefs and have a better life. When experiencing problems and limitations in our lives, we tend to think that "this is just how I am." Then we go on struggling through our days with stress, because we feel either unsafe, unworthy, un-lovable, or disconnected from others. In her book *Your4Truths,* Judy Kane explains how these feelings are often caused by unconscious, self-limiting beliefs and that they can successfully be addressed and changed. You will nod in recognition and have *aha* moments going through her book, as I had! Highly recommended reading for anyone who wants to take the reins of their own life.

— HANNE BRØTER, GRAPHIC DESIGNER AND
HEADMISTRESS AT BRØTER SCHOOL OF DESIGN

Ready for insights into how your beliefs impact your life? *Your4Truths* is for you! Judy has beautifully woven client transformations and personal experiences with information that can awaken you to what is underneath challenges in your life— personal and professional. You deserve to live your best life— read this book and begin to step into your greatness.

— ROBIN L. GRAHAM, PSYCH-K® FACILITATOR
AND INSTRUCTOR

That our subconscious beliefs shape our lives in a powerful and profound way is well known. The trick is figuring out which beliefs are in the way. Filled with many relatable client stories, *Your4Truths* is an important contribution that will enable readers to sidestep the lengthy "peeling of layers" process and get right to the root beliefs that are holding them back.

— DAWN MACLAUGHLIN, PhD, EXECUTIVE MINDSET
COACH AND CO-FOUNDER OF
RISE ABOVE PARKINSONS

If, like me, you wondered why certain goals were hard to achieve, Judy Kane's book opens the door to understanding what's really going on. For instance, deciding to just "think positive thoughts" didn't (and doesn't) work for me. I never knew why, but now I do. Judy shines a light so clearly on the real culprit—our negative subconscious beliefs. They're the origin of those negative behavior and thought patterns that, honestly, keep us from experiencing the sweetness that life offers all of us. If you're ready to discover what negative subconscious beliefs are running the show without your permission—and start to release them: read this book!

— MARIBETH DECKER, INTUITIVE ANIMAL
COMMUNICATOR AND HEALER

I so enjoyed reading Judy Kane's book, *Your4Truths: How Beliefs Impact Your Life*. It is such a wonderful reminder that we are carrying around beliefs that make no sense to keep in our lives. The examples she shares show and reinforce to us that we can choose the beliefs we want in our lives – ones that make sense and support us. This is a book you will want to read about once a year as it will remind you of beliefs you may not realize you are still owning.

— MARGARET MARTIN, GLOBAL LIFE COACH AND AUTHOR OF *THE CHATTER THAT MATTERS—YOUR WORDS ARE YOUR POWER*

Your4Truths is a book I would encourage everyone to read, because everyone has deeply buried beliefs that are holding them back. It wasn't until I had my own business that I began to be aware of beliefs "hidden" deep—beliefs that were set in the early years of my life. Most of these were not actually true, yet they clouded my efforts and regularly presented as obstacles. Judy explains these areas and their effect very simply, and the outcome of changing these beliefs is profound. You have such amazing potential—and if you are hearing an argument in your head when you read that statement, you definitely need this book!

— KELLY LUTMAN, FUNCTIONAL MEDICINE PRACTITIONER

This book is a powerhouse! It's like Judy was inside my head telling me everything I needed to hear to better understand and create my inner and outer worlds. I feel like I got a bit of "life's little instruction manual." Don't we all wish we had that sooner? *Your4Truths* are challenges I have struggled against my whole life, and now know I am not alone. There is so much clarity on these pages in understanding how the conscious and subconscious mind work, in both harmony and discord. I particularly love the 'clues' sections. I was able to self-identify and become consciously aware of patterns that I wasn't before. I now feel empowered and can see the path to alignment. Thank you for writing this book! I wish I had this book when my kids were small. It will serve me both personally and in my business. I can already tell that this book has even greater wisdom the second time around as I have already begun re-reading and feel I am having an even deeper *ah-ha* experience. I am now well on the way to creating the life I want!

— JENNIFER FLYNN, THE BALANCE MAVEN®

I loved *Your4Truths* because it gave me hope. We often get stuck in our self-sabotaging patterns and wonder how we can be free of them. We imagine how unstoppable we would be if we could break these patterns. *Your4Truths* teaches us that we can bust through our self-sabotaging patterns and limiting beliefs, and that we are in control of our life's experiences. Read *Your4Truths* and prepare for the next, most fulfilling chapter of your life!

— JILL CELESTE, MA, AUTHOR, *LOUD WOMAN: GOOD-BYE, INNER GOOD GIRL!*

Judy provides the foundation for the self-provocation necessary for real personal and spiritual growth. *Your4Truths* are applicable to every woman, man, and child.

— MICHAEL E. MULKEY, EVOLVER

With relatable stories and thought-provoking questions, Judy takes you on a journey of discovering *Your4Truths*. Each truth is simple and yet, profound. As Judy lays this out for us, the message is clear— shifting into these truths can also be simple and profound. And that is a comforting gift!

— NICOLE MELTZER, INTUITIVE SPEAKER AND AUTHOR, BALANCEDU ACADEMY

YOUR4TRUTHS

YOUR4TRUTHS

HOW BELIEFS IMPACT YOUR LIFE

JUDY KANE

Edited by
DEBORAH KEVIN

HIGHLANDER
PRESS

ISBN: 978-1-7372638-1-4
Ebook ISBN: 978-1-7372638-2-1
Library of Congress Control Number: 2021948181

Published by Highlander Press
501 W. University Pkwy, Ste. B2
Baltimore, MD 21210

Cover design: Patricia Creedon
Front cover image: Featherlightfoot/Shutterstock.com
Editor: Deborah Kevin, MA
Author's photo credit: Karl Darcy

Printed in the United States of America

To my daughters Blanton and Natalie: Thank you for being my life-long cheerleaders and supporters. I love you so much!

CONTENTS

FOREWORD

There is something remarkable happening within the pages of this book! I know Judy Kane as a friend and colleague but with her creation of *Your4Truths*, she has ventured into a new role. Judy is also an architect—a bridge builder. She built a bridge between the deepest part of the human brain—the subconscious—to how our limiting beliefs are linked with it and, further, how that shapes our reality. There is another bridge (in fact there are several!) she creates as she helps us see how when we shift our view and eventually our reality, we can more clearly see what is holding us back from experiencing more happiness, peace, and joy in our lives.

I know there are many different modalities of healing and I have experienced a wide array of them, but the common denominator in them is often when someone can have that "Aha!" moment and understands not only what has been holding them back but also shines a light on the path ahead. That path can be traveled more easily when we no longer carry the heavy burdens of limited belief, hopelessness, or despair.

The stories Judy shares are a kaleidoscopic collage of what many of us have personally experienced or have seen at play in the lives of our friends and family. It's that recognition of the experience that first draws us into the wisdom in this powerful concise book. Understanding of how the bridge to healing is formed when that light bulb goes off and we can understand a bit more about the link between what beliefs we hold and the expression of that in our lives.

I have had PSYCH-K® sessions and know from personal experience that they are effective and have helped me process and move past the "stuck places" in my own life.

As someone who works with community healing, I know that to heal a community, we must heal ourselves one by one. By doing our own work, we free up that limiting energy and can experience more energy, more creativity—more possibility in our lives and our world. We can contribute in a new way to our friends, family and community.

Enjoy the stories, ponder the similarities you may see in your own life and hopefully, you will take that courageous step and make a decision to move past your own limiting beliefs. It will then be much easier to believe from the inside out that you are safe, worthy, lovable, and connected!

Robin Saenger
Founder, Peace4Tarpon

INTRODUCTION

 You have the power in the present moment to change limiting beliefs and consciously plant the seeds for the future of your choosing. As you change your mind, you change your experience.

— SERGE KING

Writing a non-fiction book is not something I've always dreamed of doing. Every so often throughout my life, I've had ideas for a work of fiction. But this book was not on my list of goals until very recently. In fact, doing what I do now was not on my radar before 2009. Let me introduce myself and explain how I got here.

Most of my adult life I spent working in Information Technology (IT) management. My college major was statistics, and my first jobs were related to electrical engineering and statistical analysis. Then I moved to IT to become a programmer and an analyst. For those of you not familiar with this area, analysts find out what is needed by the customer, (usually) design the solution and create specifications that translate these requirements into something that a programmer can use. Then the programmers create or change applications to satisfy the customer's requirements.

The process is similar to building or modifying a house. The customer knows more or less what they want. They talk to a builder or architect or contractor who asks lots of questions to get clear on the details. These then get documented into blueprints and other supporting material that tradespeople use to make the actual changes. IT is similar—there are processes to follow and information to be gathered before the changes can be made. All of this is to let you know I come from a technical background and processes and data are in my comfort zone.

Most of my life, I did not have much exposure to metaphysical concepts or practices. I was curious about acupuncture because clearly that had worked well for centuries in Asia. I had heard the term Reiki but wasn't clear about what that actually was. That was about the extent of my exposure to energy work. I didn't disbelieve in it—I just had very limited information about it.

In 2001, I met several people who practiced a variety of energy healing modalities. I thought it was interesting but never really paid much attention to what they were doing until 2004 when my then-husband developed acute pain at the bottom of his spine. He couldn't walk, sit or do anything without aggravating it. This had been going on for several days when one of his friends asked if they could help. My husband agreed, they went off into a corner of the room for a few minutes, and when they came back his pain was completely gone. I was astounded. I had not realized this type of change was possible. I added energy work to my mental list of possible solutions if I ever needed help.

Fast forward to 2009 when the same former husband had more physical pain. The same friend offered to help, and I watched what they did that time. The modality she chose was PSYCH-K® and I could tell that this was a process that I could learn. It didn't require special gifts to sense where energy was or rely on the facilitator to intuit a solution. It was actually something I could successfully use myself. Even more interesting were the results that came from changing beliefs. The pain was totally caused by a belief my husband had. What a concept!

PSYCH-K® is a process that helps people rewrite subconscious, self-limiting beliefs into ones that support their conscious goals. It is a very fast change process, where individual beliefs can usually be changed in less than five minutes. However, many life patterns are the result of multiple beliefs that have combined to produce those patterns. Therefore, there may be multiple beliefs that need to change in order to completely change certain outcomes in a person's life.

I was so excited by the potential that I wanted to learn everything I could about it. That friend who helped my husband had a group that met on a regular basis to practice PSYCH-K®. I offered our house as the location for the meetings. Twice a month I watched as all sorts of changes were made for people in the group. Sometimes it was a physical symptom but more often the changes were about challenges people were facing with situations in their lives. In 2011 I had the opportunity to take my first PSYCH-K® workshop and I was off and running. I practiced every day and took each new level of workshop whenever that became accessible for me. I was intrigued by the process and excited by the possibilities!

I followed this path purely for the joy of learning it and the ability to make significant changes in my life and in the lives of friends and family members. If I felt nervous about doing something, I would find the belief causing that anxiety and change it. If I felt a physical symptom of "dis-ease" in my body, I would do the same thing—find the belief and change it to something that supported me.

Finally, in 2014, I decided that this was too valuable to keep to my small group that I helped. I started my business to increase the number of people that could benefit from what I do. Sometimes clients have thought it was odd that I went from IT to this, but when you examine it there are a lot of similarities. I often still need to help a client define what they really want. Sometimes they don't know what's causing the issue and we need to analyze the problem to get to the root cause. And in the end, we change or create subconscious beliefs just like programmers change or write lines of code. It's not very different at all.

The information in this book (except where references are noted) is based on personal experiences, stories that others have generously shared with me, or anecdotal experiences working with people to help them change their subconscious beliefs. My conclusions are based on these experiences and stories. Names and details within my stories have been changed to provide privacy. If you have worked with me and there is a story that sounds like you, please also know that the examples I have given are ones that could apply to many of the people I've worked with. It is entirely possible that in changing the details to maintain privacy for one client, I've inadvertently made it sound like you. In that case I thank you in advance for your understanding.

Many of the patterns and outcomes people want to change are related to some combination of resistance to four basic beliefs. Once they can change these beliefs and others specific to their own situations, they become happier, they stop subconsciously blocking success in whatever goals they have, and they generally experience a higher level of fulfillment. I call these your truths, because you deserve to believe them—we all deserve to have ease and peace in our lives.

Your4Truths:

- You are safe.
- You are worthy.
- You are lovable.
- You are connected to something larger than yourself.

In this book, we'll explore each of these truths. How does it look when you don't believe these? How does it look when you do? What are some situations that can cause your subconscious to believe them or not? It is not my intent to provide exhaustive information, but rather to give explanations of some typical reasons and some related examples. It is my hope that if you read about these it will help you understand yourself and others.

My ability to help people change the beliefs that are causing stress in their lives has been extremely rewarding. I absolutely love working with clients and hearing about the changes they subsequently see! Along the way I have learned that there are so many people living lives full of disappointment and frustration and pain, and many of them think they just have to accept that this is the way life is.

You may be reading this book because something in your life is not the way you want it to be, and you want to see what you can do about it. We all want to live lives that are fulfilling, where we feel secure and good about ourselves and our place in the world. My goal in writing this book is to help you:

1. Discover why your life plays out the way it does and to recognize your patterns.
2. Understand that if you are not happy with your experiences, you can change them going forward.

The patterns in your life reflect the beliefs you have about yourself and your environment. Those beliefs can be rewritten to support you and your goals. You can create a better life.

1

HOW TO USE THIS BOOK

To achieve the most from this book's message, read this book in the order that it is written—at least for the first time through—to understand the concepts presented, beginning with an explanation of how beliefs impact your life and some basic background information that will be referred back to in subsequent chapters. To facilitate your experience, you may download and complete the free companion workbook from the book's website (www. Your4Truths.com).

We'll explore the four truths in the order that many people choose or need to address them despite the fact that they overlap to some extent. Understanding the first truth helps the second one make sense, and so on.

Once you have a foundational understanding of the four truths, we move on to discuss the physical symptoms of stress, which could be caused by any of the four areas I describe in this book or by other beliefs—stress can be the result of all sorts of beliefs!

Finally, there is a chapter that ties all the information together and a reference section that may be helpful to you.

After you've read the whole book, you may want to go back to the chapters that resonated with you and dig a little deeper into how this may relate to your own life. There are clues in each of the Truth chapters that give examples of life patterns you might see if you believe that Truth or not. You might want to reflect on specific aspects in that chapter that relate to something in your own life. I have created some journal questions at the end of some of the chapters to help you reflect on your life and about what you want to be different. You may come up with additional thoughts and ideas. Remember—it's never too late to create something new.

When I write about beliefs, I'm referring to your subconscious, not your conscious beliefs. I want to be clear: you can't and don't choose your subconscious beliefs. Please don't use this book to beat yourself up for not being able to change behaviors and patterns you want to or have tried to change. It's not helpful to feel guilty; instead know you can improve any situation. But first you need to understand it.

If you find something that you want to change in your life, I invite you to spend time thinking about what you would rather be experiencing instead. So often people know what they don't want but haven't gotten clear on what they DO want. And it's not often easy to define. So, take the time. Imagine what the new thing would actually look like in detail and how it would feel. Sometimes getting really clear on something can be all that you need to make the change.

If you find that you need help creating the changes, there are many modalities that help people change subconscious beliefs or mindsets. I encourage you to find someone who can help you with this. You deserve to live a life that brings you joy and fulfillment—please don't settle for less.

Wishing the very best life for you,
Judy

2

HOW BELIEFS IMPACT YOUR LIFE

 There is one grand lie - that we are limited. The only limits we have are the limits we believe.

— WAYNE DYER

IF YOU BELIEVE SOMETHING, THEN THAT IS A TRUTH FOR you. Do you believe that you are safe? How would you know? I have witnessed the impacts of stress and fear in my life and in the lives of others.

As a child, I took twelve years of piano lessons. By the last two years of high school, I accompanied the Glee Club for all of its performances, played music for morning assemblies, and played processional and recessional music for many of the larger school events. I enjoyed these performances, but individual recitals were my nightmare. I felt musically prepared, but just the idea of being up there on stage with everyone watching me had me feeling nauseated as I waited for my turn—all twelve years of recitals. I worried about making a mistake or forgetting the music altogether. I just wanted the recital to be over each time I played. I can remember one particular recital—I can still visualize what I wore and where my teacher and family sat. And I distinctly recall feeling my right leg, which faced the audience, shaking violently throughout the whole performance. Clearly, I did not feel safe in that situation!

Before I understood where stress comes from and what can be done to change it, I just accepted stress as my norm. Sometimes I even embraced it as a badge of honor for how much I could endure. In my young adult years, I even thrived on how much drama I could create. I always had a story about all the things going on in my life that had to be dealt with. In my head, I said these with humor and irony but looking back I'm not so sure that's how it sounded to my friends. They probably got pretty tired listening to my litany of problems and ordeals.

It wasn't until later in life that I learned where stress comes from, it's impact on the body, and how it colors daily experiences. I also learned the role the subconscious plays in creating stress, influencing the choices you allow yourself to make, and dictating the outcomes. Along with the stress often comes self-talk caused by (and also causing) the outcomes and thus your opinion of yourself. A person who enjoys their life usually feels good about themselves, the choices they make, and the way they accomplish things in their life. An unhappy person may feel they shouldn't try certain things because they won't succeed, and generally has a critical opinion about themselves and their ability to accomplish certain goals in their life.

In both cases, people may not consider the possibility of changing their perspectives about what they should or should not try, or about their probability of success. Those things are pretty much "facts" to them.

Do you know someone who works really hard to achieve a goal and has all the skills they need to be successful, but never quite reaches the success they want? Maybe they earn just enough to make ends meet, but never more. Or maybe they never get the promotion or relationship that they seek. The effort can be exhausting and when success doesn't follow, it can make them feel defeated, frustrated, angry, or stuck. Is that what life is supposed to be: a constant struggle? That you need to work hard to achieve and if you don't get results then you just aren't working hard enough? Before I learned about the origin and impact of beliefs, I accepted that premise, but not anymore.

When you feel like something is a struggle, it is usually caused by a conflict between the conscious mind and the subconscious mind. You decide on goals with your conscious mind. It's an intellectual and creative process, based on things that you want or choose in your life. For big goals, people usually do something to prepare themselves to achieve those. If it's a promotion, then you start acquiring knowledge and skills that will be needed at the next level. If it's a trip, you might start saving money and researching all the aspects of that trip—transportation, lodging, things to see and do, what you might need to pack, or what new language you might need to learn. If you have your own business or are in a job where commissions come into play, you might calculate what it will take to hit your income goals or quotas. If it's a sport or a musical instrument, most people understand that you need to learn the basics and then practice.

But what if, after the preparation, it's still really hard to achieve the intended goal? Many people grow up believing that you need to work hard to get what you want and taking necessary steps is part of the process. Most people don't expect to learn a new language by sitting on the couch and staring at the ceiling. But if you know what to do, you're doing it, and goals still aren't being achieved and/or you are exhausting yourself in the process, something else is probably going on.

This is where the subconscious comes into play. Humans are born without instructions about how to operate in this world. To have the best chance of survival in their specific environment, they absorb rules, or beliefs, for the first six or seven years of their lives. It's how they learn to fit in, how to act, what is safe, what the beliefs are around them. Most of these beliefs come from their family, but they can also come from other influences in the child's world: church, school, neighborhood, the media. The early subconscious mind is like a sponge, soaking up the information and guidelines for making our way through this world. And much of it is crucial to survival:

- It's not safe to step into traffic.
- Don't eat food that has gone bad.
- Hot stoves and fires can burn you.
- There are customs that are important in your family or community.

Many of these beliefs serve us well throughout our lives. But most of us also pick up disempowering beliefs that end up being contrary to our conscious goals. And that's where the problems start. Because the subconscious is so much faster than the conscious mind, it's really hard to override it. It is our default way of behaving.

Let me give you an example. Have you ever driven somewhere and not been able to remember details about the drive when you get to your destination? When I'm driving, unless traffic is crazy or the weather is really bad, I'm usually thinking about something that has happened previously or planning something that will happen in the future. I'm not totally and completely actively focused on driving the car unless something alerts me to pay attention. My subconscious handles the routine driving tasks. It's the same way with our lives. You can attend a class to learn something, and when you focus you can do it the way you learned, but until it's totally absorbed and supported in your subconscious, you will lapse back into an old way because it's your default behavior. And your subconscious might not be trying for the same results that you consciously want—in fact, it might want the complete opposite. This is what causes the stress and difficulty achieving those goals. Most of the time people don't even realize that they have a belief that is working against them. They know they consciously believe things that are congruent to their goals and don't understand what the problem is.

Even if you are consciously aware that there's a challenge, the subconscious isn't easily changed with data and logic—so it's hard to correct course. The more your subconscious works against your conscious goals, the more stress you experience. Eventually your body starts sending you messages that something isn't right. These messages start off small, but if you ignore the symptoms or treat the symptoms instead of what is causing them, your messages usually become louder and louder to alert you that something needs to change. And all the time, you don't even realize it's your beliefs that are generating this havoc.

Clearly, this chaotic place is not where *you* want to be. Consider also the impact to those around you. We all have people that we love to be around. They bring joy with them into the room, and you feel better when you are with them. We also know the others—the ones who drain your energy. Maybe they regale us with all the problems in their lives or maybe they are quiet and unhappy, but something always seems to be going wrong for them. These people bring us down, and generally make us feel worse when we are with them. You've probably also had the experience of walking into a room and picking up on emotions or vibrations from those who were there. You can just tell something isn't right. How we feel affects those around us.

In my work with myself and clients, I've recognized four major categories of beliefs that keep us from living our best lives. They have to do with safety, worthiness, lovability, and being connected to something larger than ourselves. These beliefs impact the level of distress we experience, the physical symptoms of stress we acquire, our choice of goals in life, and our ability to succeed at those goals. They also impact those around us. It's a ripple effect. Every time you change a subconscious belief to support a conscious goal, your resistance is lessened, and your joy is raised. This in turn influences those around us. When you help yourself, you are also doing something good for those with whom you interact.

Maslow's Hierarchy of Needs

Abraham Maslow (1908-1970) was an American psychologist who developed theories about the psychological health of people based on their ability to satisfy certain levels of needs. His approach focused on what constituted positive mental health, which was in contrast to most psychologists at that time, who defined mental health in terms of what was abnormal. He developed Humanistic psychology which is based on the following:

> "Humanistic psychology is a perspective that emphasizes looking at the the whole person, and the uniqueness of each individual. Humanistic psychology begins with the existential assumptions that people have free will and are motivated to achieve their potential and self-actualize."[1]

Maslow's Hierarchy of Needs' original model had five levels of needs that are important to achieving full human potential.[2]

Maslow's Hierarchy of Needs Model

Source: Adobe Stock

Physiological or Basic Needs

At the very base, Level 1, the most important human needs have to do with physical requirements for staying alive (for example air, water, food, shelter, and sleep). Until these are met, it is hard to focus on the higher levels. All of one's attention has to be concentrated on getting sustainable amounts of these if they are lacking.

Next comes Level 2, safety and security. This includes more than just physical safety. People can have fears about many areas of their life: finances, emotions, physical and spiritual well-being. Fears can be logical, such as when there is an actual immediate danger to navigate. Most of us have had times when there has been a physical threat, even if it's been momentary. Car accidents or near misses are one example of a short-term danger. Living in abusive relationships, being in active combat, or residing in high crime neighborhoods are examples of longer-term dangers that some people need to react to. When fear is present, a person's safety is being jeopardized and there are physical responses to this. Stress hormones cortisol and adrenaline are produced, blood goes away from your heart and into your arms and legs, and decision-making takes a backseat to survival mode in the brain.[3] These bottom two levels are considered basic needs and are required to be met to some extent before considering the next two levels.

Social and Esteem Needs

Level 3, love and belonging, are social needs—the need for interpersonal relationships. These include family, friendships, romantic partners, work groups and any other type of connection where people give and receive affection, acceptance, love, and trust. As you would expect, this also implies a feeling of belonging within those connections.

Level 4 is about esteem and includes both your opinion of yourself and your perception of how others view your worth. Both are necessary to your ability to feel like you are important and valuable, and that you make a difference in the world.

Growth Needs

The bottom four levels are deficiency needs—ones that are necessary for humans. The fifth and final set of needs are related to self-actualization and are growth needs. They include fulfillment, feeling like you are meeting your full potential, and feeling good about who you are and what you contribute. People can have lots of different ways to feel these growth needs are being met, through creativity or relationships or tangible impacts in the world. It is not so much about what the result is, it's about feeling an authentic sense of accomplishment. People want to feel this, and according to Maslow it is actually a human need. I am writing this book to help you clear the path to meeting this need.

Childhood Experiences

The experiences we have in childhood create most of our subconscious beliefs. It is generally believed that most of these beliefs are populated by the time we are seven years old. In some areas of this book, I talk about situations where childhood traumas have been experienced. There has been extensive research done in this area, connecting specific types of trauma to behavioral and health outcomes in later life. The traumas generally fall into categories of abuse, neglect and family circumstances, and are called Adverse Childhood Experiences, or ACEs.[4]

The original study was conducted from 1995 to 1997 at Kaiser Permanente to try to understand causes for certain health conditions. They created a survey asking about ten categories of Adverse Childhood Experiences (ACEs). For each category, if a respondent said that was part of their childhood, a score of one was added. Therefore, the maximum possible score was ten, one for each category. Over 17,000 members in their HMO participated and the results revealed that about 61% of the respondents reported that they had experienced at least one of these traumas by the age of eighteen, and nearly one out of every six had experienced at least four.

The study concluded that there was a high correlation between childhood trauma and chronic health problems, mental illness, and substance use problems in later life. Subsequent studies have expanded on the definitions of these traumas and gathered more information about the consequences and prevalence of these in childhood.

It is important to know that most people experience some sort of trauma in their life. It doesn't need to be limited to definitions in any study, and it can be highly personal. Something can be traumatic for one person and not for another, even within the same family. It is also important to know that having a high ACEs score doesn't mean you are destined for poor adult experiences. Developing resilience at any stage in life can be an important way to counteract trauma.[5]

While I sometimes include trauma in my examples of how we become who we are, please understand that most people have subconscious beliefs that are limiting them, whether or not they have a history of trauma and abuse. However, it is my observation that if you do have a higher ACEs score, it is more likely that there are more subconscious beliefs that are not supporting your conscious goals.

Additionally, in spite of experiencing traumatic circumstances in childhood, outcomes can be mitigated when there are protective factors in the family or community. These are generally described as sources of support or stability. Examples include positive relationships in or outside of the family, community resources and support, and encouragement to focus on education.

Trauma can be healed in many ways, using many different approaches. Healing journeys are personal and always the person's choice as to if, when and how they address it. It's the unaddressed childhood trauma that is most difficult.

After I go into more details about each of the Truths, I will then take a little time to explain the connection between physical symptoms of stress and your subconscious beliefs. When your beliefs are causing you stress, your body is likely to start exhibiting symptoms of distress. What I have observed is that if you change the beliefs, the stress can go away. Once the stress goes away, then the symptoms will also diminish or entirely disappear. In some cases, it's been an almost immediate response and literally awe-inspiring to witness how powerful the mind-body connection actually is.

3

TRUTH #1: YOU ARE SAFE

 A ship in harbor is safe, but that's not what ships are built for.

— JOHN A. SHEDD

A FRIEND OF MINE WAS TERRIFIED OF BEES. WE DID several belief changes about this, including one where she was invisible to the bees. When we talked later about what changes she had noticed, it was fascinating to hear what she had to say. There were three changes that struck me the most. The first was that she was suddenly spending more time outside—taking walks, enjoying herself, and not worrying about potentially running into any bees. Previously, she would spend energy being vigilant about bees, but now she noticed she was just enjoying being outside. This sounded like something I would have expected, and I was very happy for her.

The other two things highlighted the unknown impacts this fear had had on her. She had been outside with her ten-year-old granddaughter. It was a beautiful day and she suggested that they get some lemonade and go sit on her deck in the backyard. Even though her granddaughter was very familiar with her house, she hadn't realized that there even WAS a back deck! My friend had spent so little (if any) time there that it was never used when the child had visited before. The other thing she noticed was that suddenly she now had lots of colorful golf shirts in her closet. She realized that somewhere in her past she had read that bright colors attracted bees and she had been unintentionally buying neutral colors for years. Once her fear was gone, her subconscious no longer needed to protect her that way. She had unconsciously started adding color to her wardrobe—and enjoying all the pretty options she now had to choose from.

Fear

Fear can keep us from enjoying many aspects of our lives and can cause us to use so much energy in avoiding what we fear. That energy could be used in so many more supportive ways! Every species has some basic survival facts that the young need to learn. Humans are no exception. We learn about gravity and moving objects and fire—all sorts of life-threatening things. The goal is to grow up and keep the species moving forward. As babies we also learn the rules of our "tribe." These vary by family and are necessary to survive and hopefully thrive in the environment we are born into.

We learn how to get along with the more powerful people in the group, because it would be dangerous to be expelled or rejected from the group. We learn how to get approval. We learn what foods to prefer and what activities and behaviors are "good." We watch our models and hear what they say to us and to each other. And much of this gets absorbed into our subconscious by the time we are seven years old. These are usually important to our well-being as a child. But by the time we are adults, some of those internal beliefs do not support us well. In fact, they can cause quite a bit of distress.

Fight-Flight-Freeze Response

Being safe is a basic human need. If this is not met, it's hard to focus on anything else. When a person feels like they are in danger, their brain switches over to the fight-flight-freeze state, and all physical and emotional resources are focused on taking one of those actions. People (and animals) have a physical response to the psychological perception of danger. They can try to protect themselves (fight), or try to escape (flight), or be so overwhelmed that they just freeze. If a situation or person is threatening to you, your reaction could be to stand and fight. This could be physical fighting, but it could also mean getting defensive, challenging the person, pushing back on the people involved in the situation, or generally showing anger or aggression or defensiveness. Or your reaction could be flight. You could physically run away, but this could also show up as avoiding the problem as much as possible. You could keep from involving yourself in the event, not commit, or be a physically or emotionally absentee parent or spouse. And if your reaction is to freeze, you may be so overwhelmed with fear that you can't take action at all. Often you can't even sort out how to respond to the threat. And you feel flooded with stress—sometimes in an ongoing manner.

Donald was beginning to experience signs of dementia. He lived alone and there were no neighbors near him. His daughters were trying to help him get diagnosed and determine what support he would need in the short term. At the end of each visit to a doctor for testing and evaluation, and during the subsequent walk to the car and drive home, he would angrily declare that he wasn't going to do any of the things the doctor suggested. He was so afraid of what the future was going to look like and of losing his independence that he went into full fight mode each time.

Fear is important and necessary for self-preservation if there is an immediate and real danger that you are facing. You want to be able to protect yourself. But most of us in the modern world are living with a chronic sense of danger due to beliefs we are not even aware of. The fear of being vulnerable, the fear of being attacked, the fear of losing everything, the fear of being alone, the fear of failure or even of being wrong—these can all haunt us in an ongoing manner. And it's exhausting! To have your systems be chronically on high alert diverts energy from your goals to your fears. It also impairs judgement. If the fear part of your brain is engaged, the judgement part has a hard time overriding that.

In these cases, you aren't enjoying your life, you aren't even responding to it in meaningful ways. You are constantly in a reaction mode that has physical consequences because the body wasn't designed to contain stress hormones on a consistent basis.

I am not sure when humans acquired chronic anxiety and stress. Animals only switch to fight-flight-freeze when there is immediate danger. As soon as the danger is over, they release that response and go back to their normal processing mode. Presumably humans were once like that too. But somewhere along the line life became more complicated.

Chronic stress

Many years ago, I was working on a project that was highly stressful. At the same time, I was in a failed marriage and sharing the house with my mother and two teenage daughters. Each of those relation-ships presented their own set of challenges. My body got tenser and tenser over time, but I didn't ever consider taking steps to release the stress. I just kept doing what I needed to do, day after day. Until the message got loud and clear. I had created a gastrointestinal situation that required five nights in the hospital. That got my attention. I spent the time thinking about what my life would look like if I continued the way I was going and making decisions about what I needed to change once I was back home. I was lucky—there were no long-term physical after-effects for me. Others aren't always so fortunate.

Many people routinely go through their days feeling mild to moderate states of anxiety. They sometimes do not even know that is happening or that it is a symptom that something needs to change. Maybe there are certain muscles that are always tense—like jaws or shoulders. Maybe they think the stress is just a normal part of being busy. Some people wear the fact that they are overcommitted, constantly multitasking, and get their best work done in the middle of the night, as a badge of honor, a sign of how much depends on them or of how busy they are. We all probably know people who say they do not have time to sleep or do other self-care activities like meditate or exercise or cook real food. They may sound like they are complaining, but they have gotten used to keeping themselves in a constant state of stress. This may be about safety or it may be about feeling worthy, which we will talk about later in this book, but it is not a healthy mindset and usually ends up being counterproductive at some point in time. It can affect your decision making, your health, and your relationships.

All of these safety beliefs show up in different ways in a person's life. But I generally notice that there are varying degrees of resistance and discomfort that are noticeable when safety is involved. This can range from a vague unease or resistance (that you cannot attribute to anything in particular) to full-blown panic reactions. They can impact how you choose your goals and how successful you are in meeting your goals. And these goals are not just about your career. Our lives are hopefully more than just our work—we have relationships, we choose ways to spend our time away from work, we choose where to live—all of these are also impacted by our subconscious beliefs about what is safe for us.

Merriam-Webster defines psychological stress as "a physical, chemical, or emotional factor that causes bodily or mental tension and may be a factor in disease causation." People tend to think of it as being caused by some external event or situation. In my opinion, stress is caused by a belief that you may not be able to successfully handle an event or situation.

When people make choices based on fear, they are choosing what to avoid—not what they want. It makes them go for the safe bets instead of stretching, growing or considering what they really WANT. Consider how this might play out.

Fear of Failure

Denise grew up in a very protective family. They never wanted her to do anything that could hurt her physically or emotionally. She didn't think she was good at sports, and apparently, they didn't either. So, they never let her try out for any team in school because they didn't want her to be disappointed or injured. They made her wear her brother's hockey equipment when she went skating decades before parents started putting helmets and knee pads on children, much to her embarrassment. Once she grew up, she moved from her native country to one where everything was new and unfamiliar. She didn't have friends there, didn't even speak the language. She made new friends and learned the new language. These new friends were big skiers, and they would all go away on weekends to ski. They walked up the mountain and skied down. The first time she went, Denise said she couldn't walk up the mountain. Because these were new friends, they didn't see her the way her old friends did. They looked at her and asked, "Why not?" And she realized it was because she'd always been told that she couldn't—there was no other reason. This was a huge insight for her, and she started challenging all the other fears she had in her life. It was a game changer for her!

Some of the rules you learn as a child are about physical safety and some are about emotional safety. Different families have different opinions on physical safety—what is risky and what is not. Some encourage mountain climbing or sky diving or contact sports. Others are constantly on alert for dangers in the environment and warn children about doing anything that could result in an injury or worse. This can cause people to avoid anything that could be dangerous, either physically or emotionally. And it can result in people choosing not to try to do new things, because they might be hurt in some way.

Other beliefs we get as a child could be about success and failure. If a child is shamed for failing at something, they are either less likely to try to do that thing again or become obsessive about being successful at everything. They may not willingly tackle anything that could risk failure. On the other hand, children that view failure as a necessary step to learning and growing have a totally different opinion of trying things until they succeed.

These are learned beliefs. When children are toddlers, they instinctively know to keep getting up after a fall so they can master walking.

But somehow that concept of failing becomes scary to many people at a young age. I have seen first-graders become distraught at the possibility of getting something wrong in their schoolwork or on a test.

Alice was so terrified of speaking in front of people that she couldn't even participate fully in audio-only telephone conference calls. As a manager in a large business, there were regular calls she had to participate in where managers across the company shared data and helped troubleshoot problems. She was able to share her department's data but got too anxious to offer any suggestions or solutions in the troubleshooting conversations. Alice knew she needed to be able to contribute if she wanted her career to grow, but she just hadn't been able to speak up. Even the *idea* of speaking up created panic. She didn't know why until asked to reflect on it. Then she remembered the incident.

She was in first grade. The teacher asked a question. Alice didn't raise her hand, but the teacher called on her anyway. When Alice answered incorrectly, the teacher ridiculed her. That was all it took— one occasion. And her life had been impacted ever since. She was able to transform that terror into a neutral response when thinking about speaking in front of others. I heard later that Alice had gone on to be successful building her career and was regularly speaking in front of groups. It was literally one belief that she changed, and what a difference it made.

The dynamic duo of fear of failure and of disapproval have created many a perfectionist, who struggle to make sure every part of what they are doing is wonderful. They deprive themselves of personal time and spend hours agonizing over the details of each project. I am all in favor of quality and accuracy—I was in IT for many years! But perfectionism is way beyond creating a good product. It causes stress because failure for a perfectionist is not an option.

Fear of being seen or heard

When I started my business, I used to get anxious just thinking about talking to a group of people. Even the thirty second intro in networking meetings was difficult for me. Eventually those got easier, and I really enjoyed the networking meetings and getting to know other people. At the end of one of these meetings, I was talking to someone who had a Web TV show and interviewed guests. She found my work interesting and asked if I would like to be on her show. My brain knew the answer had to be "yes"—it was a great opportunity to increase my visibility and was the first offer I'd had to be a guest on someone else's platform. While in my head, I felt pleased and flattered, my body had a response closer to terror. Luckily, my conscious mind controlled my voice, and I accepted her offer. I went home, created material to share, and started working on my fear. I use PSYCH-K® almost daily and am always grateful to have real-time access to such a helpful tool. I definitely relied on it to resolve my fear for this.

On the day of the show, I was confident about the experience but the closer I got to my destination, the more I noticed a little anxiety creeping up. Before I got out of the car, I did one more PSYCH-K® balance to transform that last bit of fear. When I went on set, I was so glad I had taken time to resolve my fear!

There were six cameras focused on the two chairs—each for a different live feed. And one was feeding to Bidchat, a platform which I had never heard of. My host explained that anyone watching from Bidchat could bid a sum of money to interact with people on the show. So basically, I might need to stop mid-sentence and answer whatever question they asked. A daunting prospect! The show went well, and I felt calm throughout the process. When I reviewed the recording later, I was pleased with how I presented myself, something that would not have been true if I hadn't been able to transform my old fears. I might have instead been tongue-tied and visibly shaking (just like my piano recital days). Since then, I've been a guest on many shows, and I've looked forward to each of them. They are fun for me now.

Some people are terrified of being visible to others. There can be many reasons for this. Sometimes being harshly judged or acutely embarrassed in a single painful instance can leave a lasting impression. In some families, abusive behavior is the norm and it's not safe to be seen. There are all sorts of other causes in between. Regardless of the reasons, children frequently learn that it is in their best interest to be invisible—to not attract any sort of attention. This helps to protect them in that environment but can be counterproductive later.

Many women I have worked with were abused as children. They avoid attracting attention to themselves because being unseen was a protection mechanism they used to avoid being hurt. But this protection hinders them as adults. They frequently struggle with unwanted weight, yet those extra pounds help prevent unwanted sexual attention. They shy away from speaking in front of others because it is not safe to be visible. They are stressed out if they have to offer opinions because they are afraid of being judged by others. They are intentionally "average" performers at work because they don't want to stand out.

There are a variety of ways to avoid being noticed. Whatever the causes or coping mechanisms, this fear prevents people from fully expressing themselves, being authentic, and feeling at ease.

Scarcity

Dan could never get ahead with his finances. Whenever he got a little extra, some unexpected expense would pop up. He always had just enough but never more. He grew up in a family where it wasn't nice to be greedy or to want to have too much. There are so many conflicting beliefs people have about money. Here are some that I have heard:

- You shouldn't spend money, particularly on anything other than necessities.
- You have to work hard to get money, and it certainly doesn't grow on trees.
- You are selfish if you want to spend money on yourself.
- You are greedy if you want more than you need.
- If you don't work hard for money that makes you a lazy person.
- If you have money you didn't work for, that makes you a bad

person who feels entitled and who is of questionable moral character (you don't want to be like "those people").

- You need to be charitable, but you also need to hold on to money because you may need it one day.
- Money can be evil.
- People may judge whether you're a success or not based upon your finances.

The list goes on and on. No wonder so many people have anxiety around money and create barriers to accumulating more than they need!

Scarcity can also be about other resources. Maybe there is never enough time to get everything done so that every day is an uphill struggle, with no end time for working. You probably know people who work late most days, or parents who are doing laundry at three in the morning, or colleagues who can never be on time for an appointment or meeting. These people believe that they just do not have enough time in the day to do what needs to be done.

Other people may believe that there aren't enough clients out there for everyone, and consequently they feel life is one big competition for business success. There are other resources that could be related to a scarcity mentality: not enough contacts or tools or supplies to do what you are trying to do.

Fred didn't think he could earn a living doing what he most wanted to do. He changed that belief to, "there are plenty of people out there who are happy to pay me well for what I have to offer." Afterward, he sent me this note, "Our session began at 4:15 and lasted a bit over an hour. At 5:53 pm, I got an email invitation from a national organization telling me I had been selected as one of twenty finalists and that I will be paid for my contribution! I am ready! This is amazing."

I have heard similar stories from people looking for romantic relationships. Janie didn't believe that there were any attractive, compatible men her age in her city who were interested in having a long-term relationship. No wonder she hadn't met anyone!

Believing that the resources you need are scarce creates mistrust that you can have access to what you need, which causes fear and stress. It also causes you to project that anxiety to others and becomes self-fulfilling.

Fear of Success

I've talked about fear of failure, but people can also have a fear of success. Charlie was working on growing his business. But he didn't believe it was safe to grow his business quickly. Some of the beliefs we changed were about having the knowledge and time to grow his business and that it was safe to grow his business quickly. Once we were able to identify and change that, he had five major successes in his business within two weeks. His fear had been getting in his way.

Fear of success can show up in many interesting ways. You might not always recognize that fear is running the show. If you have a fear of success or some aspect related to being successful in your business or running of a household or in a relationship, fear can show up as self-sabotage. Procrastination is one way fear disguises itself—what better way to not succeed than to not get necessary things done in a timely manner? You might put off doing something until the last minute, or you could spend your time busily doing things that aren't really going to help you move forward, or you could consistently get distracted by something totally unrelated to your goal.

Perhaps you are disorganized to the point of not being able to find critical information when you need it. I'm not talking about piles of paper or books where you know exactly where something is—that's just being messy. I'm referring to regularly spending time looking for something you can't find. Maybe you have an early meeting with an important client, and you didn't prepare the day before so in the morning you rush around, running late. When you go to grab the documents you need, you can't find them. Then the decision is whether to show up really late or show up without the information.

Do you lose important information altogether? Maybe you write a really good lead's contact information on a scrap of paper and then either lose the paper or forget you ever had it. And sure—this could happen to anyone occasionally. We all have distractions. But if it's a pattern, there's probably more to it than that.

Another type of sabotage is if you're consistently making clerical errors or omissions. Storing phone numbers incorrectly or putting an event on the wrong date or time in your calendar. Or setting up a meeting and having the notification go out with incorrect or missing information.

Clues aren't limited to sabotage. Some people I know are doing all the tasks and seeing no results. They have a resistance to getting the results and that is preventing them from reaching their goal. Many of the clients who come to me to clear blocks to success have a fear of being visible and a fear of money as the basis of that. While we may address these specific self-sabotage issues, it is important to get to the root cause as well and deal with that.

Keep in mind that the success doesn't need to be business related. Goals can be in all areas of your life: hobbies, relationships, other life plans. People afraid of some aspect of a relationship can sabotage those as well. They can create friction and drama on a regular basis until the other person gives up.

Feeling Stuck

Thelma grew up in a family that valued stability and duty over joy and happiness. She married a man that everyone said would make her a good husband, but that she never was in love with. After ten years and two children, she realized she wanted more out of life—she wanted to feel stronger emotions. She wanted to be with someone who cherished her and to be in a relationship with mutual interests and a little bit of adventure and excitement. But she also felt guilty for wanting more.

Annie had been in a loveless marriage for fifteen years. She had married a man who was just as abusive as her father. Why would she do that? Because it was familiar to her—she knew what to expect and how to cope with it. Both of these women were stuck.

People choose what relationships to be in outside of the family they grow up in. These can be romantic partnerships or friendships or business colleagues—we have all sorts of relationships in our lives. How do people pick these? It would be nice if that happened because of qualities that they admire, or because that person makes you proud of yourself, or because you know you will grow because of their impact on you.

But many people choose because of what they don't want—not what they do want. If a child grows up feeling like the world is a dangerous place—that people are only looking out for themselves— they may grow up not trusting others or having relationship issues because it is unsafe to be vulnerable. Some people pick a life partner because they have personality traits that are familiar, even if those are not supportive.

They may settle for someone safe even if love is not there. This could be because they don't want to be rejected by someone more inspiring to them or maybe because they don't think they have many options, and they are afraid of being without a partner. It could be because their family and friends approve of that choice and they don't want to risk their disapproval. And how does this play out over time? Boredom, possibly abuse of some sort, feeling like you do not matter, being taken for granted, living life stuck in a rut. That is certainly not a relationship that is interdependent, where each supports the other, where there are some common dreams and goals that are meaningful, where failures are met with compassion instead of blame, or where one is free to be their authentic self and is loved and appreciated for that.

Ending relationships can be scary because that involves change and maybe confrontation, which can be uncomfortable. [Please note: if you are in an abusive relationship, I am not encouraging you to take an action that could be dangerous. You need to consult with experts to help you navigate that.] People choose to stay in non-supportive rela- tionships for long periods of time—sometimes a lifetime—because it is too scary or too much effort to get out of them. But is that really living your best life?

Fear can influence the career you choose. If you are afraid of being seen, you won't pick a high-profile job where your actions are visible or where you have to give presentations. If you are afraid of making mistakes, you will probably pick a job that is routine and that you are positive you can master - one with little opportunity for error. These are safe picks, but do they support you emotionally over the years? Do they give you a sense of accomplishment? If you are avoiding risks, how likely is it that you will look for better opportunities when you have grown out of your current position? This keeps you stuck.

Fear also influences how you choose to spend your personal time. Does it keep you from trying out for a team or contest? Or from experiencing exciting activities that could add some dimension and contrast to your life?

If any of these examples ring uncomfortably true for you, take time to reflect. What is keeping you where you are and is there anything you would rather be doing? If you come up with something like "it's just the way I am", that is probably coming from your subconscious. If you can identify fear at the base of some of your life decisions, start objectively thinking about those choices and see if that fear is legitimate or based in faulty logic and old beliefs.

Feeling Safe

What if you saw new challenges as an opportunity to learn, grow and build your ability to succeed? What if you could be comfortable expressing yourself and your ideas to others? Can you even imagine going through the day with a feeling of peace and appreciation? Having time for self-care and for loved ones in addition to getting necessary tasks done related to your work? Being able to make decisions based on what you truly want instead of what you fear, what you are trying to avoid?

One of the main messages I have for you is that you have the right to live a life that is not controlled by fear. If your response to this concept is that you could never make enough money if you acted this way or that it would be irresponsible, take note: that is probably fear talking. People who know that there are plenty of resources available to them whenever they need them are adept at attracting what they want. People who know they have all the time they need manage to meet all their commitments, on time, and not be in a constant state of distress. People who know that balancing work with other priority parts of their life is possible and important tend to have happier relationships and feel more fulfilled. Because let's face it, when you are on the money hamster wheel, the goal amount for happiness keeps increasing—it's never enough. When you hit that goal amount and still aren't happy, you assume you must need more. But actually, it's not the money that is important—it's the way the money would make you feel. And part of that is feeling safe and secure.

Safe in Romantic Relationships

If you were able to make decisions based on what enhanced your well-being, you would be able to choose relationships that were supportive, loving and nurturing. Ones that were interdependent. The following is one way to categorize relationships:

- *Dependence* is fear-based—the belief that you won't have certain needs met if you don't have that other person.
- *Co-dependence* is the mutual fear of needs not being met if you aren't there to provide that thing to the other. I am reminded of a woman who wanted to lose weight. When it came down to changing the beliefs that would have probably helped with that goal, she was asked if there would be any drawbacks to achieving that goal. And she realized that if she lost weight, her husband wouldn't love her anymore and would probably leave her. So, she elected to not go forward with changing her weight loss beliefs. I don't know what the husband's motivations and beliefs were in this situation, but it sounds like there was some dependence of his on her being overweight. And she was depending on him to the

point where the relationship was more important than her health and self-esteem. That would be co-dependence.

- *Independence* includes an aspect of needing to do everything for yourself—not allowing anyone to do anything for you. Probably a fear of not being able to rely on others or trust them, or a need to prove you can do it all.
- *Interdependence* is where you know you are contributing and also supported by others. You feel safe to make decisions based on your own well-being, taking the impact on others into account as well—but not out of fear of rejection or punishment or deprivation. You can easily give and accept help.

Safe in Social Relationships

Think how amazing it feels to hang out with friends who challenge us mentally or emotionally or physically. These are the people that encourage us to take healthy risks or stay up with us late into the night having amazing philosophical conversations, or gently call us out when we are not being our best selves. When you are with these people, you can be your authentic self and know you are accepted and appreciated for who you are. Too many times we hang out with people who are no longer (if they ever were) compatible with us because it's safer and easier. Activities become routine and maybe even unhealthy. There is comfort in the safety of the group, but you don't feel like they really know you. However, that safety of sameness can prevent the deeper safety of being yourself and feeling good about it.

Sophie spent twenty years married to the same man, living in the same town, and socializing with the same people. They had common interests and activities in the beginning, but over time she had felt stifled by the sameness of it all. They all met on a regular basis and had the same conversations over and over. They were never interested in doing something different, and usually their get-togethers involved nothing more than eating and drinking more than was necessary. When her husband was transferred to a different state, she was sad to be leaving old friends but secretly excited that she would now be forced to create a new social network. She started thinking about how she really wanted to spend her time and also engaged her husband in conversations about what they would like to be doing as a couple. They had avoided venturing out into new friendships until the move forced their hand. And they hadn't really even been aware of it. But the move resulted in them finding new friends and interests both as a couple and individually. They got to redefine themselves in the process.

Safe in Work Relationships

In work environments, wouldn't you like to have relationships with people who can show us better ways to do things or inspire us to offer our own opinions? If you are afraid of failing, you don't pick these people because they may point out a weak area of yours. Instead, you probably choose to be with people who don't challenge you. That's not likely to bring you much job satisfaction. Looking back over my corporate career, I see times when I played it safe and other times when I took a risk by volunteering for a challenging assignment or applying for a different position. I would consistently feel bored and stuck in the safe roles, whereas the new assignments got my imagination going about how to approach them and who could I call on to help me learn what I needed to know. Just like in the example about social relationships, the perceived safety where there was low risk prevented me from enjoying my work. It was only when I felt that it was safe to take on challenges that I really enjoyed my work. Feedback from others was just a way to grow – not a threat.

As Maslow concluded, safety is a physical need for people. If you live your life in fear, the emotional and physical toll is high. The good news is you can change that.

CLUES TO ANSWER
Do you believe you are safe?

YES	NO
You are willing to try new things. You accept failures as part of the learning process.	You are afraid to try new things. You have a fear of failure.
You are comfortable and confident being visible and heard.	You have a fear of being seen or heard.
You focus on what you need to do, not on all the reasons why something is not working. You have no pattern of anxiety with specific topics.	You do not trust that you have access to everything you need (time, money, resources). You experience distress around specific topics (money, technology).
You are able to achieve your goals without undue effort.	You have difficulty achieving success.
Your life is constantly unfolding for you.	You feel stuck in some aspect of your life.

Reflection Questions

1. Are there activities or situations that cause you to feel anxious when you think about them? (a physical challenge, spending money, making a sales call, or hosting a dinner party are all examples) Can you determine what about them causes that reaction?
2. How do you feel about trying to do something new? If it doesn't go well, do you try again? If not, why not?
3. Are you comfortable when people focus their attention on you? If not, do you know why?

4. Is there any resource in your life that you feel is limited (e.g., money, time, clients, available romantic partners)? What is the belief behind that? Does that belief really make sense?

5. Do you ever sabotage your own efforts? How? Why? How would it look if you succeeded? Does that feel good to you or does it stress you out thinking about it?

4

TRUTH #2: YOU ARE WORTHY

> All too often we're filled with negative and limiting beliefs. We're filled with doubt. We're filled with guilt or with a sense of unworthiness. We have a lot of assumptions about the way the world is that are actually wrong.
>
> — JACK CANFIELD

SOPHIA IS A HIGHLY SUCCESSFUL ENTREPRENEUR. SHE HAS extensive skills, knowledge, and experience. And she normally trusts her business decisions completely. But when she rebranded her website, she went with suggestions from her web designer even though she didn't really like them. Why? She didn't feel like she knew enough about that aspect of her business and she decided to trust an expert instead of her own intuition. She was never happy with that website—instead of it being a source of joy and pride, she felt something was wrong every time she looked at it. What an expensive choice! And it ended up attracting people who were not her ideal client, because it didn't represent her.

Growing up, we create stories about ourselves. Sometimes these are about not being smart enough or good enough or attractive enough. These are all aspects of feeling unworthy to make decisions or be successful or have a wonderful life partner or just be respected and appreciated for who we are.

Once you have the physical needs satisfied from the bottom two levels of Maslow's Hierarchy (see Chapter 1) you move into frequently overlapping psychological needs. Feeling worthy is about your opinion of yourself and also your perception of the opinion that others have about you. We need to feel like we are contributing.

Imposter Syndrome

Merriam-Webster defines imposter syndrome as "a psychological condition that is characterized by persistent doubt concerning one's abilities or accomplishments accompanied by the fear of being exposed as a fraud despite evidence of one's ongoing success."

People with this syndrome consistently believe they do not deserve all they have achieved and may incorrectly attribute their success to luck or other people or circumstances. I experienced this first-hand as an IT manager. In spite of having a successful career, I wondered when people would figure out that I was seriously lacking in some skill or knowledge. I couldn't pinpoint what that weak area was, but I was sure it was there, and I would be exposed at some point in time. Not knowing what I didn't know added an additional level of anxiety to a job that was frequently high stress. Usually, it was about some highly technical aspect about one of my systems, and in retrospect I doubt that anyone really expected me to know those details. My developers were the experts in that arena, and I could easily consult with them if they were needed. At other times, it was about large projects that were completed successfully. After the relief of knowing everything had gone well, I would immedi-ately feel immense appreciation for the teams that implemented them. This was indeed justified—the teams I managed were full of skilled, motivated people and they always did a wonderful job. But I never once looked back and identified things that I did well that also contributed to the success. I felt like any congratulations offered to me were totally undeserved and I felt guilty receiving them.

Imposter syndrome is just one aspect of believing that you aren't worthy. When people believe that they can't express themselves well or are bad at math or can't generate ideas that can move a business forward, it puts stress on them whenever that skill is needed. Some don't even try to do related tasks, and others try hard but put their focus on failures only. Some spend excess hours trying to overcompensate for their perceived lack, but even becoming an expert won't take that stress and doubt away.

Many people grow up in households where nothing they did was ever good enough. There may have been a favored sibling, or it may have been that nobody did things well enough in that family to please one of the parent figures. Either way, a child's need for acceptance is important to their development. Sometimes that child just creates a narrative about how incapable they are. It doesn't really matter how the story gets there. Once they believe they aren't able to do things well enough, the consequences can follow them throughout their life. They doubt their decisions or can become perfectionists. Sometimes, people become pleasers, and never feel comfortable taking care of their own needs. We all know you can't pour from an empty pitcher, so it's not unusual for the stress to also result in physical issues of some sort.

Others are More Important

Then there's the belief of just not being enough—at all. That you do not deserve the basic right to dignity and respect as a human being. That everyone else is more important than you are, and that you need to demonstrate this by always deferring to the opinions and desires of others. It's nearly impossible to set boundaries or even determine what you want, because you believe you are irrelevant.

"I don't matter." While you may not be saying these words, you may be familiar with the feeling. Mothers model it for children who don't get to see how taking care of themselves even looks. Here's what they do see:

- You do not get enough sleep because you stay up doing household or business-related things
- You never voice your preference when picking the restaurant or activity
- You never make space for "me time"
- Your self-care routines are prioritized at the bottom of the list and therefore get dropped on a regular basis.

Maybe you sit on the sidelines and never even try to influence decisions. Or maybe you are the only one who works extra hours consistently to make sure the team is successful. Are you the one everyone just assumes will take care of all the special occasions? Or the one who always volunteers to do the things nobody wants to do—because "somebody has to do it?" You work hard to be a team player, but honestly, does it really feel like a team effort when you are doing all the work?

Phoebe knew her marriage was failing. She felt more and more trapped but dreaded starting this conversation with her husband. He was a nice man. He'd been a good match for her in many ways when they first met, but there were significant areas of conflict that were not going to be resolved. She could tell the stress of the relationship was beginning to impact her health. She had a hard time thinking that this was important enough to make the change. She finally decided that she needed to make herself her own top priority. This then let her take the steps she needed to eventually end the marriage. Even though it was hard at the time, they both ended up living happier lives apart.

Karen struggled with making her business a success. When we started digging deeper, it turned out that she had a belief that if her business became too successful, she wouldn't be able to give as much time to her family as she thought she "should." And because her subconscious primary role was to be able to do things for her family, whenever and whatever they wanted, she had difficulty even determining what amount of time she wanted to devote to her business. Consequently, she subconsciously put the brakes on every new project she thought of. Once she clarified exactly how she wanted her week to look, it was easy for her to determine when she had time to develop new offerings for her clients, and her business grew to the size she wanted.

I once worked with Paul who was unhappy in his job. He wanted to earn more money, and that was why he came to see me. But he also didn't really enjoy the culture in his department. He didn't even consider changing jobs to become more comfortable—he just wanted to be paid more. One of his new beliefs was "I deserve a job where I am supported and appreciated." He came back a few months later for another session. A new job with another company had fallen in his lap. He loved the team, was making a salary he was happy with, and was now in a management position. This time he wanted to work on his leadership skills. He had needed to believe he was worthy in order for that position to show up for him.

If you feel you aren't as important as other family members, you are probably the one running yourself ragged trying to keep everyone happy. This can mean taking everyone else's schedule more seriously than your own, cooking multiple dishes at meals to make sure everyone gets what they want, or canceling your plans at the last minute because one of them asked you to do something for them. Frequently, this behavior has become so expected for them that they feel entitled to being treated better and don't even consider that there could be a negative impact or inconvenience for you.

Anna came to me with a history of always feeling overwhelmed and exhausted. She had three school-aged children, a husband, and an aging parent. As a stay-at-home mom, every day was filled to the max keeping the house running, attending all the events for the children, transporting them to their various activities, and helping out her mother. Because Anna didn't contribute to the household financially, she felt like she needed to take care of everything else for everyone. And her family was perfectly happy with this arrangement. The problem was that she was stressed out, had no time for self-care, was getting irritated with people, and found very little pleasure in her life. And she didn't even realize that life could look different! While she came because of the lack of energy, we ended up addressing beliefs about deserving to have support, to set boundaries, and to prioritize her own needs so that she could actually take better care of the others. There were a few other beliefs we worked with, but the results were really positive. When she started having more self-esteem, her family started to appreciate her more. They were able to negotiate some expectations together that gave her time to replenish her own energy and still meet the real needs of her family.

Accepting Gifts, Compliments, or Help

Another way your lower priority can reveal itself is if you have difficulty accepting gifts or compliments. This may result in you feeling compelled to over-reciprocate. How many friends do you have that can't accept a favor without paying you back immediately? Or who deflect compliments? Or who always insist on paying the entire check when you go out? It's wonderful to be generous, but when there is no balance, it's frequently a subconscious belief that they aren't good enough to receive the favor or the gift. The people I know who are like this become really anxious when you try to insist on paying—it stresses them out. Or if you loan them a cup of flour on Monday, they show up with the flour AND a cake on Tuesday. In some relationships, it can cause hurt feelings when someone is unable to accept and enjoy a gift that is offered.

If you don't think you are important, it is also hard to accept help from people. It's even harder to admit that you need help. Maybe it's because asking for help means you will be inconveniencing someone. Or accepting help means you can't take care of everything by yourself. Either way, it makes your life harder and doesn't allow others to make something a team effort or to at least show support or affection for you.

Negative Self-Talk

Just as fears can impact your choices, self-esteem can do the same thing. Do you constantly notice what you do wrong and ignore all the things you do well? Do you feel uncomfortable even using the word "deserve" or "proud" when talking about yourself? If so, you probably have some subconscious beliefs that have limited your major life decisions.

My first "job" was tutoring math. I started this in the summer after tenth grade and continued tutoring summers, nights, or weekends until I was thirty and starting my family. I didn't like to teach groups, but I loved the individual sessions where I could explain a concept in as many ways as necessary for that one pupil to understand. As corny as it sounds, I really loved seeing that light bulb switch on in the eyes of my students. I honestly only had one child that I never was able to get through to. I'm not sure what the impact of aptitude is when you're talking about basic math, even though I know there are tests out there that claim to measure that. I'm more inclined to believe that some people just learn in such a different way that the right explanations are never provided. But I do know that many of my students *thought* they weren't good at math when we started. I can remember being so frustrated with some of the mothers who dropped off their daughters because they said in front of those children that it wasn't surprising that the child needed tutoring because they themselves were never any good at math either. I didn't know about the subconscious back then, but I did understand that statements like that had an impact on confidence and performance.

My mother always said that people generally live up to your expectations. I think she intuitively understood the impact of beliefs. As a teenager it would have been rude to point this out to the parents of my students, but I remember several of those children being absolutely gleeful when they finally realized that they could do math as well as anyone else. Some even found out they enjoyed it! I like to think some of them chose careers that were more science oriented because of their new confidence. I'm pretty sure they would have avoided careers like that if they had continued to believe they were poor at math.

Your opinion of what you are capable of influences your career and extracurricular choices. If you aren't confident about your skills, you aren't going to pick a career where you think you will fail. I know creative people who don't recognize their own talent, and natural salespeople that say they could never sell, brilliant strategists who never make suggestions, and people with the personal traits to be good leaders who only feel comfortable following others. Why don't they see what others see? It's those subconscious beliefs that were acquired so long ago.

Negative self-talk isn't limited to business. It can affect your social life or your success in hobbies or sports that you might otherwise enjoy. What has been your process for making new friends? Do you immediately rule out people who seem "out of your league?" Have you done the same thing with romantic partners? For many people their whole demeanor changes if they think someone they are talking to is more "worthy" than they are. They can get tongue-tied or babble nervously. They may not be able to make direct eye contact. And the signals they send to the other people cause reactions that just reinforce the belief. I'm not advocating for aiming to be with people just because they are popular or powerful. Sometimes they don't have the behaviors that you admire. But to not feel comfortable communicating freely with people who truly interest you because you feel "less than" is limiting who you choose to spend your time with and the growth opportunities that may result from those relationships. If you're constantly telling yourself that you're not good with people or you're clumsy or you're really bad at doing something, you are letting those beliefs limit who you're with and what you do.

Entrepreneurs

Even though some people have been high achievers in school and corporate jobs, they can still struggle with their confidence—especially when they decide to have a business of their own. Confidence in being worth what they charge can be a really big thing. If you are uncomfortable telling someone your price, apologize for your price, or have a pattern of negotiating to a lower price, you probably have some beliefs that what you do is not good enough to charge higher prices. Wouldn't it be wonderful to know your strengths, be comfortable charging reasonable rates, and be proud of your accomplishments?

I know many entrepreneurs who had former successful careers in the corporate world. Some of them had beliefs that they could never make as much money on their own as they did by working for someone else. Changing beliefs to knowing your potential is unlimited when you own your own business, and that you can make lots of money doing what you love, has made a big difference for many of them.

Other common beliefs I've seen that hamper success in business center around giving yourself permission to run your business as you see fit. Giving yourself permission to change your business model, or set your own hours, or establish boundaries sounds obvious if you are an entrepreneur. And yet so many of us try to live by rules we didn't intentionally create. Knowing that you can trust yourself to make good decisions, set your own priorities, be successful and still have a healthy work-life balance are important to building a life with less stress, more joy, and a feeling of accomplishment.

Shame, Doubt, and Guilt

Once you have made choices about your life goals based on your beliefs about what you deserve to have, is everything fine? Maybe not if those beliefs are limiting you. Because even in the daily flow, your beliefs influence how you show up for your family, what your interpersonal relationships are like, and how you succeed in your career. Sometimes people grow up with tremendous shame or guilt about things that happened to them in their childhood. Children are quick to blame themselves for situations they had no control over. This can lead people to doubt themselves, have difficulty making decisions or repeatedly revisit their decisions.

Talia had done a lot of work with herself to get over the negative emotions she had after the end of a twelve-year marriage. The split had been costly both emotionally and financially. She knew she was okay about the end of the relationship, but every so often emotions would come up that she couldn't identify even though the divorce had happened several years earlier. One day she was in a workshop and the activity was to sit still and listen for messages about whatever topic she wanted. She chose this situation. After a while, she tapped into overwhelming emotions of sadness and regret.

She knew it wasn't about her former husband, so she worked with a partner to find out more about what this was. She finally realized that she was mourning the time she had lost in that marriage. She felt like she has wasted what should have been some of the best years of her life. That is what had kept her going back over and over again to the whole topic, and what she'd never realized before. Once she knew what the issue was, she was able to change those beliefs. Then that voice inside of her stopped scolding her for spending her time and money that way. She stopped revisiting the situation and felt more at ease and happier inside.

These are all signs of low self-esteem:

- Letting other people take credit for your ideas or you actually giving others the credit.
- Constantly apologizing to others for everything: for things you do, for how you look, for what's in a report, for how the coffee tastes, and even for other things you have no control over.
- Allowing people to talk down to you or over you.

Here's what I heard from my friend Maribeth:

"I think we did at least one or two sessions on my ability to do videos. I would spend so much time setting up the video that I wouldn't get around to creating the video or when I got to do it, I was completely flustered. I got lost in the minutiae of, "How does my hair look? Is the lighting right? Do I have the right background?" Over time I have noticed that I'm not so concerned about the perfection of the setting. I find that I have more ability just to do an off-the-cuff Facebook video. And actually, even more significantly, I started doing weekly healings in one of my client groups. Also, I wanted to do interviews but didn't think I knew anyone to talk to. And now I'm on a schedule where I'm interviewing one person each month. We do the interview, and we get it up on YouTube, and then it becomes a blog. It's cool to break it down so that it becomes little segments that I can use. The synchronicity is so interesting because all of a sudden people are showing up whom I'd love to interview. Before I was like 'I don't know how I'm going to interview, because I don't know anybody.' It's really been interesting. I'm sure that came from whatever we did to release some of the beliefs about how it's supposed to go and how it's supposed to happen and what I'm supposed to look like."

Releasing all those beliefs about how you should be can not only feel liberating, it can let you access so much more that you want—things you were blocking before.

Stereotypes

Stereotypes can be present in your subconscious beliefs even when you don't consciously believe in them. While these can impact people in all possible categories, among my clients I have most often seen women who were sabotaging themselves because of stereotypes that women aren't supposed to be highly visible, successful, or assertive. Their "real" place should be at home, tending the family and the hearth fire. When this belief is present, any attempt to have a successful career or business is met with huge resistance from their subconscious. They notice this by how hard it is to get anything done. Then they tell themselves that you need to work harder to be successful, you need to work crazy long hours, you need to know more, you need to have more luck or be better to get ahead. But it can actually just be guilt that you aren't doing what you are "supposed" to be doing. I actually found my business stalled for a while when I turned seventy. In trying to figure out what was going on, I traced it back to my grandmother's belief that it was unseemly for a woman (especially one my age!) to even think about working, much less having a successful business of my own. I should instead be staying at home and being available to take care of my grandchildren in a much bigger way than I was doing.

Worthiness and Self-Trust

Imagine how it would feel to trust yourself to make good decisions, to be able to set clear boundaries with people, to appreciate yourself and know that others value you and your contributions. How empowering would that be? If you value your own contributions, you are more likely to experience feelings of collaboration and teamwork when working on goals with others.

What does it look and feel like when you believe you are enough? You are authentic—you feel free to express what you think, what you want and what emotions you are experiencing. You can easily walk up to people you want to know better and feel comfortable starting a conversation with them. You can host an event and not spend your time worrying about anyone else's opinion about what you have provided or how you look or if the location is good enough. You try out for clubs or teams or promotions and the main emotion you feel is curiosity about what will happen instead of sitting at home thinking about all the reasons you don't deserve to achieve this goal.

Wouldn't it be rewarding to be able to model for others what being confident looks like. When things don't go the way you'd planned, to easily move past that—maybe learn a lesson from it, but not beat yourself up over it or dwell on it? If your self-esteem is healthy, you also don't blame others or events for things that happen in your life. You can easily take responsibility for what is yours to control. And you don't need to feel responsible for things that are not in your control. See what a difference your beliefs can make?

CLUES TO ANSWER
Do you believe you are worthy?

YES	NO
You are confident about your ability to do things. You know it's okay to not know everything.	You experience imposter syndrome. You attribute your successes to other people or to luck.
You prioritize your own needs and boundaries. You are comfortable and appreciative accepting help, gifts or compliments.	You put other's needs in front of your own. It's hard to accept help, gifts or compliments.
You know when you have done a good job. You are proud when that happens and can celebrate your successes.	You engage in negative self-talk. You never stop to feel proud of what you did.
You easily make decisions. You look at new opportunities with excitement.	You consistently feel doubt, uncertainty, shame, or guilt. It's hard to make decisions or you repeatedly revisit decisions.

Reflection Questions

1. Do you usually attribute your successes to luck and/or to others? What do you feel proud of about yourself?
2. Do you have a pattern of rearranging your priorities or schedule to accommodate others?
3. Is your task list full of items you didn't prioritize or negotiate—just things that need to be done by "somebody"?

4. If someone offers you a compliment, can you simply say, "Thank you"? or do you diminish it by saying it really wasn't worth paying attention to?

5. Pay attention to your self-talk. What is there more often—criticism or cheer-leading?

TRUTH #3: YOU ARE LOVABLE

 Your task is not to seek for love, but merely to seek and find all the barriers within yourself that you have built against it.

— RUMI

FREQUENTLY, THERE IS AN OVERLAP BETWEEN NOT FEELING worthy and not feeling lovable. Many people are either looking for love they haven't found yet or are missing love in an existing relationship. It has been my experience that if someone isn't in a fulfilling loving relationship and if that's something that they want, then it's a good idea to see if they love themselves first. Almost always the subconscious does not love and accept themselves in these situations. If you don't love yourself, how can you have an authentic loving relationship with someone else?

Harriet was in a relationship that was often disappointing and sometimes humiliating. Her boyfriend demeaned her in public and had a wandering eye. After several years of trying to make the relationship work, she finally started working on her beliefs about herself. As she made changes, the relationship ended. She was at peace with the choice. She realized that she loved herself enough to expect a relationship where she was cherished and respected for exactly who she was. Staying in that old relationship had made her feel terrible about herself.

Lack of self-love can result in shame about parts of yourself. You may constantly tell yourself what is unlovable about you. Maybe it's about body image. Maybe it's about personality attributes that you consider to be flaws. Maybe it's about things you won't even admit to yourself—they stay hidden deep inside because you are only able to love the parts of you that are "perfect." This can make you unhappy with yourself and thus probably with all around you. It also can result in you acting like someone else. You might only display what you think others want to see in order to be loved or do whatever you can to ensure that others love you. In this case, you are constantly hiding your real self and that is exhausting!

How do people end up feeling unlovable? As I've said, most of our core beliefs get there by the time you are seven years old. Different people can take away different messages from the same set of circumstances, so that two children treated mostly the same in the same family can come away with different beliefs. But generally speaking, from what I've seen and read, if children feel loved and accepted and valued as they grow, they are more likely to love themselves and develop loving relationships. If they are unloved or loved only when they behave in certain ways, they are more likely to lack love and trust later.

Consider the following scenarios that could give a child the belief that they are not loved:

- A child was unwanted from the beginning. This could be because they were an "accident," or the result of violence, or came at a bad time financially for the family or were blamed for other events that they had no control over.
- Another child in the family is actually valued more. Many families are blended now. Parents can be biased in how they view their own children vs their stepchildren. In some

families a son automatically has more value than a daughter. Sometimes middle children don't have the special place that first children or last children have. Sometimes older children or children in families where someone has special needs are expected to do more to help out and can feel they are treated differently. Sometimes because children are treated differently (for a variety of reasons) they may create the story that they are loved less, even when that might not actually be true.

- Evidence of love may be absent. A caregiver may not know how to express love because they don't feel it themselves. This can be a generational problem, of course, that perpetuates itself. If the parent can't model it, how can the child acquire it? Or caregivers can be too busy to nurture the children, either because they have to work multiple jobs to provide or because their work-life balance or priorities are skewed.

These could all be true in relatively stable family situations. Imagine how much worse it is when there is abuse, neglect, or other trauma.

Unhealthy Relationships

Many of my clients have come to me from a coaching program that helps women find the love of their lives. They have usually had a series of relationships that followed a specific pattern. I discovered that until they worked on the relationships that they had with themselves, their relationships with others were unlikely to change much. Start with loving and appreciating yourself. And I think this is the biggest, most important love belief. When you don't love yourself, you attract people who don't really love you much either. Once you love yourself, your whole approach to others changes. I call it your vibration, but even if you can't relate to that, you certainly know when you are with someone who is feeling good about themselves as opposed to someone who is putting up their guard and setting barriers in place. Those barriers are put there by your subconscious when you don't think it's safe to be vulnerable. If you don't love yourself, you can't trust others to love you, so the barriers go up to protect yourself. In addition, our response to others teaches them how to treat us. So expecting to be supported and respected and valued will attract people who provide that for us. You can't expect that from others if you don't feel it for yourself.

Once the self-love is in place, your relationship with others is easier to figure out. If you don't love yourself, you are constantly doubting that anyone else could possibly love you. And this can lead to behaviors that either test a relationship or dismiss what you need for yourself. You can see this in child-parent relationships, between partners, or in any other type of interpersonal relationship.

Lucy had had two long-term relationships, and both had been disastrous for her emotionally and financially. She was pretty sure subconscious beliefs were part of the problem. She had been so mistrustful of potential new relationships that she stopped dating despite wanting to have the marriage of her dreams. She defined what she really wanted and discovered some beliefs about herself that had created barriers. She changed her beliefs about being lovable and that there were indeed men worthy of her. She got clear about what she wanted in a relationship, and then her world began to change. Within a couple of weeks, she was asked out by three different compatible men. She felt stunned at how her beliefs influenced something so seemingly out of her control. It wasn't a surprise to me—changing her willingness to try again and her trust that there were good options available for her also changed how approachable she was to others.

Sometimes we expect issues with someone, and that expectation actually causes the problem—it's self-fulfilling. Frank had anxiety around money. He was always stressing out about the possibility of not having enough to live on. He was afraid to spend money on anything because of this. His husband was the exact opposite. He enjoyed spending money when they had it. Once Frank's beliefs about money changed for him, he was still concerned about this disconnect within the family. Once he changed his belief that there was conflict there, he found out that they could sit down and map out a strategy that worked for both of them. This made a huge difference in their ability to provide for themselves for the future and to have productive conversations about their budget.

Sometimes people create conflict in their relationships because of beliefs they have about themselves. We tell ourselves stories to explain what has happened to us, and then our brain finds ways to prove that those stories are true. This sometimes can be extreme. Some people become manipulative in an effort to make people prove their love, either by behaving badly to reassure themselves that they are loved or by requiring certain behaviors or services or gifts as proof.

Candice had some old beliefs about men only wanting to be with her for physical reasons. She didn't feel valued after a relationship became sexual and had a pattern of failed romances. She was in a relationship that was in trouble. No matter what her partner told her, she couldn't trust that she was important to him beyond sex. After she changed beliefs about being cherished for herself, their whole relationship changed.

The concept of unconditional love is challenging for many. How many times have you heard someone say, "If you loved me you would (or wouldn't) do (fill in the blank)?" I have had many clients whose perceptions were that their parents withheld love as punishment or only gave it as a reward. This doesn't allow them to trust in love and it is also what they have accepted as love—a conditional relationship. So "love" is used to influence what another person does. But unconditional love is the opposite. It's there regardless of the behavior. It doesn't mean approving of everything another person does—you can love a person and not like something that they do—but the love is there for the person no matter what. This concept can be expanded beyond individual relationships. Many spiritual doctrines are based on loving others in a general and unconditional way. Sadly, it looks like we have a long way to go for this to be the norm, but it's certainly something to strive for in our personal relationships and a worthy long-term goal in general.

What is the impact on your life when you feel unlovable? People make choices based on their beliefs, so what type of partner are they likely to choose? Do they pick partners who are unable to provide love and support? Do they choose friends that are never that close? Do they even have friends? What about how they spend their personal time? Is it something meaningful or just a way to take up time in the day? Regardless of the relationship you are looking at, if you grew up where love was withheld, it may be a challenge for you to feel or express love for or trust in others. Resulting relationships can be empty or difficult.

Often people have come to me with relationship concerns within their marriage. Once they started believing that they deserved love and support and appreciation, they saw clear shifts with their partners. The change in belief about themselves caused them to behave and relate in a different manner with their spouses. And then of course the spouses responded differently to them in return. I've seen this turn out two different ways. With some, the relationship improved significantly, and they were able to rebuild the marriage successfully. With others, unfortunately, the changes made it clear that it wasn't in either person's best interest to continue in the marriage. And while the ending of a relationship is not something to celebrate usually, it was a positive and healing step for those clients to be able to bring closure to what was not working and begin to move forward in their life, attracting more compatible and affirming people.

Sometimes trust in love can be so broken that a person retreats into a self-imposed loveless existence—they have totally given up on the possibility of love. This could show up as reclusive behavior or as being unpleasant to be with. The pain of not being loved is so great that they push people away to avoid any possibility of connection and failure or abandonment.

Madge grew up with severe abuse as a child. As an adult, she had two abusive marriages and then decided that she just couldn't do that anymore. She put on extra weight to avoid unwanted attention, developed a very tough demeanor, and rudely discouraged all potentially interested men. I met her fifteen years after her last marriage ended.

She'd been doing lots of self-healing, but still suffered from PTSD at times. As much work as she had done, there were still some old beliefs operating in her subconscious. She was able to change those and believe that she was valuable and lovable, and that it was safe to be in a loving relationship. A few months later she told me she was open to being in a new relationship. I heard later that she had indeed found a man who provided the type of relationship she wanted.

Difficulty Expressing Yourself

Sometimes I ask people how they feel about a situation or a person, and they aren't sure how to answer. The concept of identifying their feelings is actually foreign to them. They spend so much time hiding from themselves, or trying to be what they thought others wanted, that they have a difficult time getting in touch with their own emotions. Even when they can identify their feelings, it can be hard to express them to others. It keeps relationships from becoming as deep and meaningful as they could be.

Molly had a husband and three sons who were in their early twenties, two of whom still lived at home. She didn't feel that she was important to any of them. She didn't know that was the issue at first. She only knew that she was consistently unsure of being supported or even loved by them. One of the ways this showed up for her was her reluctance to bring up sensitive issues because she didn't want to cause conflict. She changed her beliefs about being able to speak her mind freely and to trust that the relationships were solid and loving. This let her address sensitive topics with her husband more confidently and her relationships became better all the way around. She noticed that her children started asking about how her day was and offering to help out around the house. Her unease around them had caused the relationships to feel strained and uncomfortable. Once she trusted that the love was there, her whole demeanor changed, and they all started to interact differently with her.

Trusting your relationships and being clear about how you feel are necessary when it's time to initiate difficult conversations. And every relationship has times when those are needed. If you aren't able to have these, things get swept under the rug, remain unsaid, and tend to allow distance or resentment to build up over time.

During the pandemic, many people found themselves sharing space nonstop with other family members, subject to frequent interruptions. Amy was one of these people. She loved her husband dearly but needed time to focus and plan, in order to expand her business. He always seemed to want to share something important to him at the wrong times for her. She didn't want to hurt his feelings or appear uninterested, but the interruptions were impacting her ability to focus and get her work done. Changing beliefs about it being okay to negotiate boundaries and explain what she needed made a huge difference in their ability to work in the same house.

Poor Self-Care

Lack of self-love can also show up as neglect of your physical, emotional, intellectual, or spiritual needs. We touched on this some in the chapter about being Worthy. It's important to feel like you deserve to prioritize these needs. But sometimes you may not even feel like you deserve to take care of yourself. I have talked with so many people who put all their focus on business or family or something outside of themselves, and still feel empty. If they loved themselves fully, they would make the necessary time or effort to tend to themselves too.

Eve had struggled with her weight all of her life. She also had experienced a variety of chronic health conditions since childhood. Normally I can help people get to the root cause of physical symptoms in a straightforward way, but we weren't making the progress we both had hoped for. Finally, we started checking in to see if her subconscious believed she deserved to be healthy—and it didn't! All those years, for whatever reason, she had these underlying beliefs that she was supposed to be sick and unhealthy. And these were tied to loving herself, knowing that she was whole and perfect just as she was.

Self-Love

Love is an essential psychological requirement for a happy, fulfilling life. It gives you a sense of support and of value. To know you are lovable, you first need to love yourself. What does self-love mean? If you love yourself, you eat nourishing foods, and get adequate sleep and exercise. You live in a space that is clean and pleasing to you. You pay attention to your emotional state and respond to times when you need to be more understanding or supportive of yourself. You recognize when your mind needs stimulation or when your soul needs centering or when you need to take time to be creative. And then you act on this knowledge. You only engage in relationships that are supportive of you. You create healthy boundaries. You know how you feel and can communicate your emotions easily to others. If a difficult conversation is needed, you are able to initiate it. When you need help, you can ask for it. You are comfortable creating space in your life to take care of your own needs.

The certainty of love is a powerful thing. It lets you know that someone is always there for you. There is peace and comfort in knowing you have a soft place to land when you need it. When you love others unconditionally, it's loving them for who they are.

Being lovable means knowing that others can love you the same way. Knowing you are lovable lets you be your complete self, without hiding parts away. You know that with unconditional love, all of you is loved. You can be honest about your faults and errors, knowing that these are accepted as parts of the larger you and that we all have lessons to learn and improvements to make. You know that your complete self is still wonderful and lovable, regardless of what you perceive to be failings. So then let's imagine yourself knowing you are loved. You feel special, valued, your heart is full of joy. There is a smile on your face and your forehead is relaxed. Your body is open and relaxed because you are being open about who you are—you don't have all that stress of pretending to be someone you are not. Where are these emotions in your body? Take a moment to actually get into this feeling and see what comes up for you. Imagine how it looks, how it sounds, how it feels.

My friend Suzanne Moore shared a story in her book, *Hang on Tight! Learn to Love the Roller Coaster of Entrepreneurship*, that illustrates how a situation can turn out when there is love and trust in a relationship. Early in her career, she wanted to invest a significant amount of money in her business. She had put off making investments for several years because she felt she needed her spouse's agreement and she assumed he would have objections. It was only after she had done some work on her mindset that she realized she was expecting resistance instead of appreciating the fact that he approached expenses in a way that was different from and complementary to her own. She brought the subject up knowing that he would need time to process the various aspects before deciding if he thought it made sense or not. Once he was able to do that, he fully supported the investment. Whenever they see a situation differently, she says "I go back to what I believe to be true about him, 'He loves you. He wants to do the right thing just as much as you do. He needs time to process your perspective on this.'" [6]

This is a beautiful example of how a relationship can look when there is potential for conflict and when both people accept and love each other as they are.

CLUES TO ANSWER
Do you believe you are lovable?

YES	NO
Your relationships are based on trust and open communication.	You have a pattern of unhealthy relationships.
You can identify emotions that you are feeling and express those to others. You are comfortable initiating difficult conversations.	It is difficult to identify or express your emotions. You cannot comfortably initiate tough conversations.
You take the time for self-care. You are able to establish healthy boundaries.	You neglect yourself. You are reluctant or unable to prioritize your own needs.

Reflection Questions

1. Do you have a pattern of unhealthy relationships? Look at the common attributes of these and think about what those could mean, related to your beliefs about yourself.
2. Do you have difficulty identifying the emotions you are feeling? Can you express your emotions to others?
3. Can you calmly initiate difficult conversations with others? Or do you keep the problems to yourself and build resentment?
4. What do you do to take care of your own physical, emotional, intellectual and spiritual needs? Is it enough?
5. How well do you set boundaries? Are you able to honor and communicate these effectively to others?

6

TRUTH #4: YOU ARE CONNECTED

 The least movement is of importance to all nature. The entire ocean is affected by a pebble.

— BLAISE PASCAL

HAVE YOU EVER BEEN SOMEWHERE AND FELT OUT OF place? That's an experience that most of us have had. It's uncomfortable, isn't it? You feel like you stick out or are being judged by everyone there. It can be stressful. Most of us try to limit the occasions where we expect that to be the case. But what if you felt like that all the time? Imagine how exhausting and unempowering that would be!

Odd Duck Syndrome

Many people regularly feel isolated and disconnected. It may be within their inner circles of friends and family. It may only be true for them in a larger context, and some people feel separate from the whole world —like they and their actions have no impact on the world whatsoever.

You might feel completely misunderstood, possibly even excluded from family activities, maybe even like an outcast. Sometimes it's blatant that a child was not wanted. Or it could be the result of family structures and situations. Sometimes it's more subtle, but the message is still clear to the child. "You don't belong here." Or, "You are not like us." And if this is their take-way, whether intended or not, it makes navigating life very challenging for them.

I relate to people who feel different. My parents separated before I was a year old, and my mother moved from Illinois back to Virginia to live with my grandparents until I was five when my mother remarried. My stepfather didn't really appreciate sharing my mother's attention, and we always had an uneasy relationship. I think it was largely due to this that I never really felt like I belonged. And because my preschool years were spent without many interactions with children, I wasn't socially prepared for kindergarten—I really only knew how to relate to adults. This caused a different set of problems building relationships at school. As most children do, I made up stories in my head to explain the world to myself. And for much of my life I would try to figure out what other people were looking for and act the part. My life was not a disaster—I had a family, good friends, a robust social network, a successful career. But every so often something would happen that made me feel like I just didn't fit in or wasn't wanted. I didn't realize I could change that until I learned about changing subconscious beliefs. I've changed several related to this since then. Every so often some connected emotion will pop up in a particular situation. But now I recognize those for what they are and change them.

You might feel like you operate in a bubble or feel you are constantly judged. People may ignore or put down what you have to say, ridicule you, or bully you. Maybe it's difficult to walk into a group —especially if they are strangers or you don't feel like there is any common ground between yourself and others. There are lots of places and ways this can happen. Maybe you grew up feeling like there was just something "off" in your relationships within your family, it didn't even have to be extreme. At the other end of the spectrum, you could have suffered from neglect or abuse during childhood and never developed a sense of trust in relationships. Or you could be a member of a minority group and experienced the trauma of being "other" on a daily basis due to this. You could be a military veteran who is no longer part of the unit they were in, or a refugee from a war zone. All of these are examples of how you could feel disconnected.

Remember Maslow's Hierarchy of Needs? It's a psychological need to feel like we belong. When we don't, there is a critical missing piece in our lives. People can cope with this is various ways. You might pretend to agree with others in order to fit in, or defiantly declare your opposition to others on a regular basis, or completely withdraw. Pretending to agree keeps you from feeling authentic and can also create situations where you follow along and participate in behaviors that make you like yourself less. Defying the norms is a way to self-exclude and avoid the pain of being rejected. Withdrawing could mean that you no longer even hope to belong, and you are not willing to risk being open to forming connections.

Empathy-Challenged

If you feel disconnected, it may also be hard for you to understand how others are feeling or thinking. When making decisions, you may rarely consider the impact of your actions on others or the environment. Your goals would be more about what impacts you directly. This would make it difficult for you to empathize with others. Because you never felt understood, you really don't understand what others might be feeling. This makes it difficult to nurture your children, have loving relationships with others, and create successful relationships in work or social settings. It can impact your career if you are unable to empathize with employees or peers. Leaders or team members with no empathy don't develop trust with each other and that can impact morale, creativity, problem solving and productivity.

Sometimes this disconnection isn't general—it is limited to a small number of people. I have had many people come to me because a particular person was challenging to be with. I remember one man who had a prickly relationship with a stepson. John really wanted to get along because the tension was putting a strain on his marriage, but everything the child did seemed to rub him the wrong way. We focused on beliefs about appreciating the child for who he was. That made all the difference! John was then able to see all the funny and lovable things about the child and the irritations lost importance— that change in perspective helped create a connection between the two that could be built up over time.

Sometimes I see the disconnection in work groups. There can be individuals that only see the differences between themselves and some of the others. There is mistrust about intentions and competence. This has such a negative impact on group dynamics and productivity. When people can assume positive intent, and be open to hearing everyone's perspective and suggestions, magic happens. People feel good about how they are contributing, they feel heard, they feel like they are truly part of something bigger and better.

In my former life as a manager, sometimes bad feelings came up between different work groups. Something would happen that would cause a problem, then everyone would start blaming other people or other teams for not doing something they were supposed to have done (or for not doing it correctly). As part of the problem resolution, we would analyze the root cause and implement processes and procedures to prevent a recurrence of the problem. Almost always, when the finger pointing was at the team level, it came down to assumptions that each team had about what the other team was supposed to be doing. Defining roles, expectations and boundaries was always the first step and it was usually eye-opening to all involved. Once we came to agreement about those, putting preventive measures in place was easy.

When you think that you, or some group that you are a part of, are different from another, it can be hard to consider things from that other point of view. And that is a limiting belief that makes collaboration and being part of something bigger difficult.

Connections are vital in our lives. It's impossible to exist without impacting those around us, but sometimes people feel so isolated that they don't recognize where these connections are. The stress of feeling alone or ostracized can be paralyzing. The stress of feeling at odds with others is equally draining. If you feel unsupported or constantly judged, it can have a huge impact on where you put your focus and energy and how satisfied you are at the end of a day.

Feeling Connected

How wonderful would it feel to know that your home was your soft spot to land, to know that within your family you are part of a loving, supportive unit that is really looking out for the best interests of all, even on cranky days? Imagine walking into a group you don't know and being perfectly at ease and just curious. Not feeling the need to pretend to be someone other than yourself? Knowing that you can find something in common with anyone you connect with? Being confident that you have gifts that can make something even better? These are the empowering beliefs that help you feel connected.

I set up a pilot group of three people to launch a new workshop. I was delighted because the group seemed to be diverse in many aspects: they didn't know each other, their businesses were totally different, and they were geographically separated from each other. I congratulated myself because this would give a variety of perspectives on how to improve the workshop before offering it to a wider audience.

About a third of the way through the seven weeks this workshop spanned, they made me laugh. They asked how I had been able to find three people who had so much in common! They noticed that they all faced similar challenges in their businesses and had some of the same basic beliefs that were holding them back. Clearly these people did not feel isolated—they looked for the connection within the group. Each actively looked for ways to empathize with what the others were going through. It was a happy supportive group.

The fourth truth is that you absolutely are connected to something bigger than yourself. You impact others. You matter. You matter on a practical and individual level, and also on a broader level. What happens to you has an impact on those around you. Our behaviors and decisions always have impacts on others. The more grace we give ourselves and others and are able to relate to each other, the better we can collaborate and get positive results.

Our emotions spread, for better or worse, to the people we directly interact with and then indirectly on to the people that they interact with. Think of a ripple in water when something disturbs the surface. It's a similar reaction. You've probably experienced the impact of group enthusiasm or group fear. It's something that feeds on itself and spreads through the group and then beyond. So how you feel has consequences far beyond yourself.

Loneliness is not a natural state for humans. The basic human need to belong is strong, and the lack of this can keep you from living a full and satisfying life. The fear of being kicked out of the group can cause people to do things they would never do on their own. Being "other" keeps you from making contributions that would help you feel fulfilled and improve the world around you.

You deserve to feel like you belong, that you are an important part of a whole, that you matter. And when you do, you also have a better sense of who you are, because you know you are accepted and appreciated for that. This gives you a voice. It lets you be your unique self, to be comfortable with yourself and around others. You deserve to feel in control of your life and to enjoy that life to its fullest. You can stand taller knowing that you are being your authentic self and at the same time are part of a bigger picture.

If you look around you, you'll notice that in nature everything is interconnected. None of the animals or plants live in isolation. They all have an impact on each other. They work in harmony with each other to keep everything in balance. If you feel disconnected from Nature, you don't recognize the impact your behaviors are having on our world. Burning the forests, polluting the air and the water, depleting farming soil, none of these things seem pertinent to a person who feels separate from the natural world. How did humans get so disconnected from nature and from each other? Look around at all the stress and pain this causes. The sense of being "other," the isolation some people feel, the depletion of resources we all need in order to survive and thrive. These could all change if enough people recognized our interconnections.

CLUES TO ANSWER
Do you believe you are connected?

YES	NO
You are comfortable and authentic interacting with others. Your decisions are made with an awareness of their impact on others.	You feel like you are "other than" or that you operate in a bubble.
You easily relate to others and look for ways to connect with and understand them.	You don't understand or appreciate others.

Reflection Questions

1. How easy is it for you to understand and appreciate someone else's position?
2. Do you tend to look for differences or commonalities when interacting with others?
3. How often have you felt like part of a highly functional group? Of a dysfunctional group? What were the differences between these groups?
4. How often do you consider the impact on your family, community or environment when you make a decision?
5. Are you happier collaborating or competing? Why?
6. When you are problem-solving with others, is winning the most important thing to you or do you try to find solutions that are win-win for all?

7

___

PHYSICAL SYMPTOMS OF STRESS

 I find that when we really love and accept and
APPROVE OF OURSELVES EXACTLY AS WE ARE,
then everything in life works. It's as if little miracles are
everywhere. Our health improves, we attract more
money, our relationships become more fulfilling, and we
begin to express ourselves in creatively fulfilling ways.

— LOUISE HAY, *YOU CAN HEAL YOUR LIFE*

WE'VE TALKED ABOUT FEELING UNSAFE, UNWORTHY,
unlovable, and disconnected. All of these beliefs create stress. Most
people agree that stress can cause your body to display physical symptoms. Many chronic diseases are attributed to stress, headaches are
commonly associated with it, and there are lots of other symptoms
that are connected to beliefs. I think of the body as an instrument
panel, letting you know when something isn't going well. If beliefs
cause stress, and stress causes symptoms, then it stands to reason that
if you change the beliefs and the stress goes away, then the symptoms
will go away, too. The body has amazing powers to heal itself.

I have on numerous occasions been in meetings or at events where someone near me will say they have a migraine and are going to have to leave. I usually offer to help and so far, everyone has accepted the offer. In less than ten minutes, they can change beliefs enough for the migraine to be totally gone, so that they can stay at the event and fully participate.

I have also seen people experience physical symptoms based purely on calendars. You probably know someone who says they always get hay fever or the flu or a cold at a certain time of the year. And they do, but it can be more related to their belief than anything in the air.

One of my biggest challenges is to not point out the problem when I hear people make statements about having to live with aches and pains and mobility issues as they age. "What can you expect at my age?" "Growing old is not for the faint of heart!" Talk about limiting beliefs! If you can relate to those statements, please find out why you have the pain or the issue. You can probably change it and not expect to have to live with it for the rest of your life.

Mark had symptoms of responses to pollen and ragweed. Every fall and every spring, his nose would start to run, and his eyes would start to water. This would last two-to-three weeks each time. We worked on these several times, finding beliefs that were contributing and then changing those. Eventually the symptoms went away, and he stopped dreading those seasons. Some of his beliefs were tied to the calendar, "I always get hay fever" whenever that season came around. Others were tied to the world being safe. These can be beliefs you pick up from your family—it may even be generational to react to seasonal changes. I have also seen situations where an unpleasant event happened at the same time someone was eating a particular food (or breathing pollen!) The subconscious linked the substance to the emotional pain and created an adverse response whenever it detected that substance. People are often surprised when they learn they don't have to live with these symptoms.

Bruce H. Lipton, Ph.D., has written extensively about the impact beliefs have on the body.[7] His early work in epigenetics, once disregarded, is now becoming more mainstream. What he found is that cells behave differently depending on their environment, and that most "dis-eases" are not because of the genes you inherit but because something in the cell's environment turned on a switch that enabled that disease. As he writes in *The Biology of Belief*, there are a small number of diseases that are caused by a single gene. Most diseases are correlated to some combination of genes and environmental factors. And he is careful to point out the difference between cause and correlation. A cause is the reason something happens. Correlation occurs when two things occur at the same time, but one thing is not necessarily causing the other.

He also cites fascinating studies about the placebo effect and the nocebo effect. Basically, the placebo effect is when you have a positive medical outcome because you believe the treatment will help you. In trials, some people are often given pills with no ingredients that could impact the condition, known as placebos. The people frequently have an improvement in their condition, even when there is no ingredient that should have made a difference. In contrast, a nocebo produces unwanted results because the person believes those will happen. You could develop some of the side effects listed just because you read about them—it's the power of suggestion. In some studies, people actually experience the unwanted side effects even when the pill they took was a sugar pill.

In Dr. Lipton's work, he also gives examples of situations beyond medications. For instance, a controlled experiment with knee surgeries was conducted at Baylor School of Medicine and published in 2002 in the *New England Journal of Medicine*.[8] The lead author, Dr. Bruce Moseley, conducted the trial to better understand a particular knee surgery. There were three groups of people all with the same knee problem. One third of the people received the actual procedure, one third received a less extensive surgery and one third just had an incision with no other procedure. Much to everyone's surprise, knee improvement results were similar between the three groups. This was presumably because of the beliefs the patients had, because there was no medical explanation for it. In a different story, a man was given a very bleak prognosis about cancer and told he only had a few months left to live. He died about when the doctor predicted, but an autopsy showed that the cancer was very limited and not the cause of death. Again, this is presumably because the patient believed that was when and why he was going to die.

These are all examples where you can identify the belief. But I work with lots of people where that belief is not so easy to find. For instance, several people have wanted to lose weight and discovered that their subconscious was holding on to the "weight" because they were "waiting" for something in their lives.

Barbara had twenty pounds that she just could not lose. She had tried everything she could think of, with no success. She had relocated with her young son several years earlier to take care of her mother, who had been diagnosed with a terminal disease. Much of her life had been put on hold since then. When we talked, her mother had passed on and her son was graduated and out on his own. We discovered that her weight was related to her "waiting." She created beliefs that it was now her time to be her own priority and to get moving on her own path. She called me about six weeks later. She hadn't done anything intentionally different in terms of exercise or diet, but she had lost over ten pounds and was very happy about that.

Research shows that prolonged stress produces higher levels of cortisol, which negatively impacts your immune system and increases inflammation in your body. As we know from the results of the ACEs study, children who experience violence, abuse and neglect have a much higher probability of developing chronic conditions such as depression, asthma, cancer and diabetes in adulthood. They are also more likely to engage in risky behaviors such as smoking and alcohol abuse. These outcomes are attributed to the stressors they experienced early in their life.

It is important to know that chronic stress is not limited to people with high ACE scores, and not everyone with high ACE scores experiences high stress. But if you have beliefs, for whatever reason, that are causing ongoing stress, your body is being impacted. It will begin to send signals to you that something needs to change. If you ignore those, it will usually try to get your attention by either creating additional symptoms or intensifying those that you have. Treating the symptoms without addressing the root cause will have the same effect as ignoring them: your body will continue to try to get your attention.

Anita Moorjani wrote in *Dying to be Me* about how she was dying from cancer and lapsed into a coma. Her description of her near-death experience is captivating. During that event she learned that we need to love ourselves. What happened after she came out of her coma was remarkable. Within weeks, her tumors and other cancer markers all disappeared. "I can't say this strongly enough, but our feelings about ourselves are actually the most important barometer for determining the condition of our lives!"[9]

When I work with clients on changes related to physical symptoms, it always amazes me if the symptom goes away immediately even though I've seen this happen many times. It's not always that fast, but when it happens it is breathtaking to be reminded of how strong the mind-body connection really is.

I occasionally see people with mobility issues such as not being able to fully turn their head or to raise an arm higher than their shoulder. Once the related belief(s) has been found and changed, there is usually an immediate change in their ability to move.

Melanie suffered from severe sciatica and was sometimes unable to even leave home due to the pain. This had been going on for years but was getting progressively worse. She changed beliefs related to being supported, to anger and fear, and to trusting her own strength and resilience. Several days later she was experiencing no pain for the first time in months. It was hard for her to believe a condition that seemed so established could go away that quickly.

Secondary benefits

What are secondary benefits, you might ask? It's when there is some payback to you from the condition you are trying to change. You may not want the condition, but it's giving you something you don't want to give up. Maybe it's letting you avoid something you don't want to do. Maybe it's letting you do something you wouldn't otherwise feel right doing. But in some way, there's a benefit even if the primary condition is not. This is usually something we try to identify up front when people are trying to change a habit, and it applies to all sorts of beliefs, including the ones that are related to physical symptoms.

Several years ago, I went on an Alaskan cruise. One of the excursions was zip-lining. We had to walk up a fairly steep hillside to get to the first jump-off spot, and I had a terrible time doing that because I was out of shape and needed to stop to catch my breath. (To be fair, where I live in Florida is flat and I rarely encounter stairs. It would have been hard to prepare for that incline.) It was extremely embarrassing to me for everyone to be cheering when I finally got where I needed to be. (That's another belief—instead of appreciating the support and well wishes of everyone, I immediately was uncomfortable to have been that obvious about the struggle I had. These beliefs crop up everywhere!) Soon after I got home, I developed a pain in my right hip that I could not budge. After quite some time trying on my own to resolve it, I enlisted the aid of an acupuncturist, then a gifted massage therapist, and, finally, a holistic chiropractor. Still no consistent improvement! It finally occurred to me that as much as I want to move easily and freely again, I didn't want to take a chance of being that embarrassed again AND I didn't want to do the necessary work to get into shape. My hip pain was my excuse to do neither.

How do you know what needs to change? When I work with clients, I use muscle testing to identify the messages. People such as Louise Hay have written books that list common conditions and likely causes. But often it is highly individual—just a message the body is trying to communicate. The important thing for you to know is that you can do something about unwanted physical symptoms—they are not something you just need to accept.

Reflection Questions

1. Do you have physical "messages" from your body where you treat the symptom instead of identifying the root cause? (an

example might be always getting a headache during or prior to a particular activity)

2. For any unwanted physical symptom or constraint that you experience, think about if there are any benefits you get from that.

8

WRAP IT UP

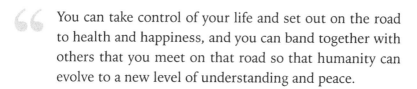
You can take control of your life and set out on the road to health and happiness, and you can band together with others that you meet on that road so that humanity can evolve to a new level of understanding and peace.

— BRUCE H. LIPTON, PH.D., *THE BIOLOGY OF BELIEF*

PULLING IT ALL TOGETHER—FEELING SAFE, WORTHY, lovable, and connected—feels like taking blinders off. You can see who you truly are and appreciate yourself and others, without being emotionally highjacked, constrained, or held hostage. These are not separate and distinct areas of your life—fear can impact relationships, self-esteem and loving relationships impact each other. Fear and self-esteem can keep you from being successful. The lack of belief in one of the truths can impact your belief in another.

Take a look at what is going on in your own life. And look at how you feel about yourself before looking at your relationship with the world around you. Do you feel safe and secure with yourself? Do you trust yourself? Do you appreciate and value yourself just as you are? Do you love yourself unconditionally even when you may have done something you don't particularly like? Do you feel comfortable and at peace with yourself? These are the places I like to start. Once the answers to these questions are "yes", then you can move forward with your beliefs about what and how you interact with your world. You can look for patterns that indicate you may be limited in some of those as well.

You deserve to live a life where you feel safe, worthy, lovable, and connected—where your choices are based on what you want instead of what you fear. The goal of this book is to help you understand that you have the power to choose how to live your life. You don't need to be boxed into limited options because of emotions and beliefs that you don't even recognize are controlling you.

Freeing your subconscious mind of the beliefs is the first step. Then you stop telling yourself the conscious stories that you have created about yourself because of what has been. Often coaches and therapists are important allies to help identify patterns and effective ways to change the behaviors and stories that have become habits. Once the subconscious and conscious mind are working together to achieve the new goals, the stress is transformed and that has positive results in the physical body. All that stress can cause inflammation, aches, pains, and other symptoms. But when the stress goes away, the symptoms will also begin to disappear. So not only are you freeing your mind, you are freeing your body.

We've looked at how feeling safe or unsafe can impact your life. Fear influences your stress levels, your choices, your success and often your physical well-being. Then we looked at how feeling worthy and feeling lovable play into those same aspects of your life. Finally, we saw that these can all influence how much we feel connected or isolated.

Many will say that because most of these beliefs start in childhood, it's just the way you are going to be. But that does not have to be true. There are a variety of ways to start changing those beliefs and consequently to start changing your life.

The stories in this book are about people who wanted the change badly enough that they kept looking for ways to accomplish that. And the consequences have been amazing for them. From freedom to build a successful business, to the ability to make order out of tasks that used to be overwhelming, to bodies that no longer had the aches and pains that plagued them, life altering changes were made. Many gained the ability to be clearheaded when dealing with typical problem areas like money, relationships and careers.

Everyone deserves to believe these four basic truths: you are safe, you are worthy, you are lovable, and you are connected to something bigger than yourself. Knowing this allows your subconscious to support you while you go about the business of building a rewarding, engaging and joyful life. What if every day you felt supported in your endeavors? If you got to follow your dreams and have them come true? If your normal state was in the flow? If you were truly enjoying your life instead of just going through the motions? If you never had to feel stuck, overwhelmed or in a rut again? If new ideas inspired you instead of intimidated you?

Can you imagine living in a place where most people believed these for themselves and about others? Would we be nicer to each other because we felt better about ourselves? Would we be more helpful because we knew that there was no scarcity of opportunities, so we could collaborate instead of compete? If enough people chose to do this, would crime go down? Would health indicators get better? Would our environment begin to reverse some of the damages that have been inflicted on it? Think of what all the creative ideas could produce, if people weren't afraid to speak up. A life is a terrible thing to waste being limited in so many areas. Make a decision to design your life to be the way you want it, right now. Don't settle for less.

When people feel safe, they contribute and openly collaborate, when they feel valuable, they appreciate themselves and others, when they feel lovable, they are compassionate, and when they are aware of their connections and impact on others, they are more intentional in their behavior.

Now more than ever, it is important to start raising our vibrations individually and collectively. We need to be conscious of our interconnectedness and aware that our decisions and behaviors impact others and our environment. We need to understand that our success depends on collaboration, compassion, appreciation and respect. There is so much fear and division now in our daily lives. It's not sustainable—it's time to change.

Reflection Questions

1. Are there any aspects of your life that you wish were different?
2. What's keeping you from changing those?
3. What would you rather have instead? (Be detailed.)

ENDNOTES

[1]McLeod, S.A. "Humanistic." *Simply Psychology*, December 14, 2015. https://www.simplypsychology.org/humanistic.html.

[2]McLeod, S.A. "Maslow's Hierarchy of Needs." *Simply Psychology*, March 20, 2020. https://www.simplypsychology.org/maslow.html.

[3]Northwestern Medicine. "5 Things You Never Knew about Fear." Northwestern Medicine. Accessed August 28, 2021. https://www.n-m.org/healthbeat/healthy-tips/emotional-health/5-things-you-never-knew-about-fear.

[4]"Adverse Childhood Experiences (Aces)." Centers for Disease Control and Prevention. Centers for Disease Control and Prevention, April 3, 2020. https://www.cdc.gov/violenceprevention/aces/.

[5]Jane Stevens (PACEs Connection. "PACEs Science 101 (Faqs) - Positive and Adverse Childhood Experiences." PACEsConnection. https://www.pacesconnection.com/blog/aces-101-faqs.

[6]Moore, Suzanne Tregenza. *Hang on Tight! Learn to Love the Roller Coaster of Entrepreneurship*. Baltimore, MD: Highlander Press, 2121.

[7]Lipton, Bruce H. *The Biology of Belief: Unleashing the Power of Consciousness, Matter & Miracles*. Carlsbad, CA: Hay House, Inc., 2016.

[8]Moseley, J. Bruce, Et Al., Author AffiliationsFrom the Houston Veterans Affairs Medical Center (J.B.M., S. Horng and F.G. Miller, D.T. Felson and J. Buckwalter, P. Nathan and Others, B. Balikagala and Others, et al. "A Controlled Trial of Arthroscopic Surgery for Osteoarthritis of the Knee: Nejm." New England Journal of Medicine, July 11, 2002. https://www.nejm.org/doi/full/10.1056/NEJMoa013259?query=recirc_curatedRelated_article.

[9]Moorjani, Anita. *Dying to Be Me*. Carlsbad, CA: Hay House, 2014.

RESOURCES

"Adverse Childhood Experiences (Aces)." Centers for Disease Control and Prevention. Centers for Disease Control and Prevention, April 3, 2020. https://www.cdc.gov/violenceprevention/aces/.

Lipton, Bruce H. *The Biology of Belief: Unleashing the Power of Consciousness, Matter & Miracles*. Carlsbad, CA: Hay House, Inc., 2016.

Lipton, Bruce H. *The Honeymoon Effect: The Science of Creating Heaven on Earth*. Australia: Hay House, 2014.

McLeod, S.A. "Humanistic." *Simply Psychology*, December 14, 2015. https://www.simplypsychology.org/humanistic.html.

McLeod, S.A. "Maslow's Hierarchy of Needs." *Simply Psychology*, March 20, 2020. https://www.simplypsychology.org/maslow.html .

Moore, Suzanne Tregenza. *Hang on Tight! Learn to Love the Roller Coaster of Entrepreneurship*. Baltimore, MD: Highlander Press, 2121.

Moorjani, Anita. *Dying to Be Me*. Carlsbad, CA: Hay House, 2014.

Moseley, J. Bruce, Et Al., Author AffiliationsFrom the Houston Veterans Affairs Medical Center (J.B.M., S. Horng and F.G. Miller, D.T. Felson and J. Buckwalter, P. Nathan and Others, B. Balikagala and Others, et al. "A Controlled Trial of Arthroscopic Surgery for Osteoarthritis of the Knee: Nejm." New England Journal of Medicine, July 11, 2002. https://www.nejm.org/doi/full/10.1056/ NEJMoa013259?query=recirc_curatedRelated_article.

Northwestern Medicine. "5 Things You Never Knew about Fear." Northwestern Medicine. https://www.nm.org/healthbeat/healthy-tips/emotional-health/5-things-you-never-knew-about-fear.

Stevens, Jane. "PACEs Science 101 (Faqs) - Positive and Adverse Childhood Experiences." PACEsConnection. https://www. pacesconnection.com/blog/aces-101-faqs.

Remember that you can download a free PDF workbook to use along with this book at www.Your4Truths.com.

ACKNOWLEDGMENTS

I have been so appreciative of, and amazed at, all the support and encouragement I've received during the process of writing and releasing this book!

Thank you, Robin Saenger, for being my good friend, for writing the lovely Foreword, and for introducing me to Peace4Tarpon and the ACEs study.

Thank you, Robin Graham, for teaching me in all those PSYCH-K® workshops and being such a generous source of wisdom and knowledge.

Thank you to all of you who provided blurbs and feedback before this final version was complete. You have no idea how happy you each made me.

To all the lovely people who provided me with stories, cheered me on, and helped me launch and celebrate the completion of this book, I've been so humbled by your support and enthusiasm.

A special thanks goes to those who were by my side throughout this whole process. The members of my writing cohort (Cheri Andrews, Nicolette Blanco, Jill Celeste, Maribeth Decker, Nicole Meltzer, and Suzanne Moore) provided knowledge, inspiration and encouragement. Pat Creedon designed a lovely cover. Suzanne Moore, in addition to being a cohort member, helped guide me through the launch process, which is much more complicated than I ever realized. Finally, and especially, thank you to Debby Kevin and Highlander Press, for being my friend, my editor, my publisher, and my educator throughout this whole process. Your patience and knowledge were very much appreciated, and the cohort structure was brilliant!

ABOUT THE AUTHOR

Judy Kane, a PSYCH-K® facilitator, helps people identify and release subconscious beliefs that keep them repeating unhealthy, stressful patterns. The shifts her clients experience result in them finally achieving what they've longed to—with ease and comfort. Judy also hosts workshops and presents in group sessions, conferences, and on podcasts. Originally from Richmond, Virginia, she lives near Tampa Bay, Florida, usually with a rescued cat or dog (or two) as part of her household. *Your4Truths* is Judy's first book. To learn more about Judy and PSYCH-K®, visit www.alignedconsciousness.com.

facebook.com/alignedconsciousness
linkedin.com/in/judykanepsychk

ABOUT THE PUBLISHER

Highlander Press, founded in 2019, is a mid-sized publishing company committed to diversity and sharing big ideas thereby changing the world through words.

Highlander Press guides authors from where they are in the writing-editing-publishing process to where they have an impactful book of which they are proud, making a long-time dream come true. Having authored a book improves your confidence, helps create clarity, and ensures that you claim your expertise.

What makes Highlander Press unique is that their business model focuses on building strong collaborative relationships with other women-owned businesses, which specialize in some aspect of the publishing industry, such as graphic design, book marketing, book launching, copyrights, and publicity. The mantra "a rising tide lifts all boats" is one they embrace.

facebook.com/highlanderpress
instagram.com/highlanderpress
linkedin.com/in/highlanderpress

Made in the USA
Coppell, TX
16 August 2024

36091683R00066